SIGNS OF LIFE

NURTURING SPIRITUAL GROWTH IN YOUR CHURCH

JAY SIDEBOTHAM

Library of Congress Control Number: 2022944186

Scripture quotations are from the New Revised Standard Version of
the Bible, copyright ©1989 the National Council of the Churches of
Christ in the United States of America.

Psalm quotations are from the Book of Common Prayer.

© 2023 Forward Movement
Second printing, May 2023

Forward Movement
inspire disciples. empower evangelists.

SIGNS OF LIFE

NURTURING SPIRITUAL GROWTH IN YOUR CHURCH

JAY SIDEBOTHAM

FORWARD MOVEMENT
Cincinnati, Ohio

What People Are Saying

"Everyone wants the secret to reversing church decline. There is no shortcut, but in *Signs of Life*, Jay Sidebotham lays out the clearest path you will find. The RenewalWorks team has spent a decade researching, testing, and guiding thousands of congregations, and I am so grateful that Jay has now literally written the book on spiritual vitality and what it takes to ignite a fire for God in the heart of our churches."

—The Rev. Canon Stephanie Spellers
Canon to Presiding Bishop Michael Curry
Author of *The Church Cracked Open* and *Radical Welcome*

"Devoid of any time-bound and shallow gimmicks, this thin volume is actually an expansive atlas, a collection of maps that tells us both candidly where we are and how in hope to get where we want to go when we decide to be led by God to living together in Christ. This book will renew Christ's Body the Church for the sake of the world!"

—The Rt. Rev. A. Robert Hirschfeld
Bishop, Diocese of New Hampshire

"*Signs of Life* is written by a pastor for any person, lay or ordained, who cares about congregations. Jay Sidebotham's decades of experience in parish churches, as well as his vulnerable witness that developing 'more programs' is not the same as deepening faith in Jesus Christ, grounds this work and makes it both practical and beautiful. ...This book affirms the truth that attending to tasks that hold up basic, common-sense, and faith-filled practices will strengthen a local church. The warmth of leaders (clergy and lay), getting people moving, embedding scripture in everything, empowering others, and caring for the entire local community are honest-to-goodness keys to the kingdom."

—The Rt. Rev. Thomas James Brown
Bishop, Diocese of Maine

"*Signs of Life* is a must-read for anyone in church leadership within the Episcopal Church. Whether you are clergy, a professional lay minister, a vestry member, or serve as an usher one Sunday a month, this book will challenge and strengthen you and your ministry for the better."

—Jerusalem Greer
Manager for Evangelism and Discipleship
The Episcopal Church

"For nearly a decade now, Jay Sidebotham has helped Episcopal parishes rediscover their first loves and grow in spiritual vitality. In *Signs of Life*, he distills the wisdom gained from that work into an accessible and inspiring single volume that should be required reading for every vestry, search committee, priest, and Episcopal seminarian. His relentless hope for the future of God's church has inspired me in my own ministry, and the work of RenewalWorks has been transformative in the life of every parish I have served. I know it will continue to bear much fruit."

—The Rev. Ryan Fleenor
Rector, St. Luke's Episcopal Church
Darien, Connecticut

"Through stories, interviews and insights from a lifelong passion to help people grow spiritually, Jay Sidebotham shares all that he's learned about how to take intentional steps on the journey of faith and help others do the same. RenewalWorks isn't a program; it's a pilgrimage. It isn't one thing to add to an already busy life and full church calendar; it points us in the direction of what matters most of all."

—The Rt. Rev. Mariann Edgar Budde
Bishop, Diocese of Washington

"*Signs of Life* is a deeply insightful guide to leadership and parish vitality. It would be hard to measure the impact this work can have on the spiritual and numerical growth of your congregation."

—The Rev. Chip Edens
Rector, Christ Church
Charlotte, North Carolina

Contents

Introduction

Is Flat the New Up?

About two dozen rectors gathered for an annual clergy retreat, a gathering that was to last for several days. Most of that time would be facilitated by a guest presenter, but the time always began by going around the circle. Each church leader talked about what had been going on in their congregation over the past year. Along with successes, the leaders described challenges facing their congregations. These were often referred to as "war stories." In recent years, the war stories included declining attendance, challenging budgets, clergy and staff running on fumes, cranky parishioners, battles with vestries, and so on. Church is not for the faint of heart. In the circle, several leaders boasted about the ways that they weren't doing worse than last year. After a few of those accounts, members of the group began to wonder: *Is flat the new up?*

In the Episcopal Church, the ministry of Forward Movement began in the 1930s at a time of challenge and decline, not only in the church but also in the wider culture as well. The spirit of the Great Depression had spilled over into the church, and leaders were struggling to maintain the institution. During a discussion at the General Convention of the Episcopal Church, someone rose and said: "We have to hold the line!" To which someone else responded: "We don't need to hold the line. We need a *forward movement.*" Out of that conversation, the ministry of Forward Movement was launched, based on the premise and promise that the church *would* move forward with a focus on spiritual practices. Specifically, revitalization would come with reading and reflecting on scripture, bolstered by a deepened prayer life, led by persons committed to discipleship. It was a vision of the spiritual journey unfolding not only on Sunday mornings but throughout the week. The story of the genesis of Forward Movement prompts us to consider what might be the forward movement for the church these days. *Do we see any signs of life?*

Welcome, then, to a discussion of how the church might *move forward*, with clear-eyed consideration of the various challenges facing congregations as well as a celebration of those practices that contribute to spiritual vitality in congregations. We call these best practice principles "signs of life." The concepts and the stories presented in this book emerge from a ministry called RenewalWorks. RenewalWorks is a concerted effort to make spiritual growth the priority in Episcopal congregations and to build cultures of discipleship in those congregations. This book is intended to offer an honest assessment of the current state of the church and, at the same time, highlight signs that give us hope for the days ahead. The book is written free from illusion that there is any quick fix. Nor do we propose a prescriptive focus on programmatic solutions. Renewal in the life of the church requires a *culture change* in many cases, and that kind of change does not happen overnight. What you have in this book is simply hopeful confidence that it can happen. After all, with God all things are possible (Matthew 19:26).

This ministry of RenewalWorks began outside the Episcopal Church, at a large nondenominational church in suburban Chicago. Willow Creek Community Church was, by all measures, a model of success for congregational life. The parking lot was so big you could lose your car, so numbers were placed on light posts to help people remember where they parked. Few Episcopal churches face that challenge. But amid all the apparent success, senior leadership at Willow Creek came to realize that while they had been successful in welcoming newcomers in a seeker-friendly environment, they were not sure that people were actually *growing* in their spirituality. Their spiritual *hunger* was not necessarily being addressed. Many active members were dissatisfied and looking to other communities for spiritual *renewal*. This led the leadership to engage a market researcher to find out what was going on in the hearts of parishioners. Where were these people on their own spiritual journeys? What moved them? What shaped their religious practice? What stood in the way of spiritual growth? The church created an online inventory to give an accurate picture of where people in the congregation were in their spiritual journey. Out of data gathered, they identified several best practice principles for vital congregations. But would that kind of learning apply to Episcopal congregations?

Starting the Work of Renewal

As rector of an Episcopal church north of Chicago, I got wind of the research emerging from Willow Creek, beginning with the learnings that vital congregations are ones that are deeply engaged with scripture. Based on that research, our parish began a yearlong process of reading the Bible. From September to May, we made a commitment to read scripture, front to back. Our education programs for adults and children focused on a passage of the week. Many in our congregation were reading scripture for the first time in a long time. Many had no idea of the trajectory of scripture. Did Abraham come before Moses? Where did David and Isaiah and Daniel and Jeremiah fit in the picture? There was indeed a sense of renewed spiritual interest in the parish, based on this experience of biblical exploration. People loved it.

With that initial success behind us, I decided to go deeper in exploration of this process from Willow Creek, offering the online inventory and subsequent workshops that served as a discernment tool. I came to think of it as spiritual strategic planning. We learned a lot about where members of our parish were in their spiritual journey. We got some clear ideas of where we would like to go.

In some respects, it was a bumpy start. The language from this more evangelical church was strange and in some cases offensive to our Anglican congregants. That led us to begin a process of translation and adaptation to make the material Episcopal/Anglican-friendly. The process included material that inquired into the meaning of the sacraments, as we discovered there was great hunger for deeper understanding of the meaning of Holy Baptism and Holy Eucharist.

The process led to a new level of engagement with questions of spiritual growth in the parish. Some people resisted that kind of focus. Others embraced it. Neighboring congregations began to express interest. A group of congregations in the diocese took on the work. Churches around the country heard about it. I began to get invitations to lead presentations, which spoke to me of the spiritual hunger in Episcopal congregations. That hunger seemed to be an important sign of life, a desire for more even if the roadmap was uncertain. Indeed, our research has since shown that Episcopalians have a deep hunger for spiritual growth, though folks are not always sure how to go about addressing that desire. Clergy don't always know how to address that need either. It became clear that there was a need to focus more intentionally on what this process had to offer. I was not able to do that and continue to run a church at the same time. So, I resigned my position as rector and launched a ministry in partnership with Forward Movement called RenewalWorks, which began on July 1, 2013.

The ministry of RenewalWorks seeks to help congregations (and their leaders) know where congregants are in their spiritual journeys. Based on the data gathered through spiritual inventories, leaders and congregants can chart a course forward. The process has revealed that Episcopalians go to church for all kinds of reasons. Some go simply because it's what they have always done or because it is what their family has always done. Some come for the music. Others come for a sense of community, to be with people who have become friends and companions on the journey. Some come to savor the beauty of a particular building, others to be involved in a particular outreach ministry. All of these are good reasons for coming to church. But our work embraces a lofty but vital aspiration: *the primary reason for coming to church is spiritual growth,* by which we mean growth in love of God and love of neighbor. All other reasons (music, fellowship, service) grow out of that commitment to spiritual growth.

Stages Along the Way

That pathway of spiritual growth is represented in RenewalWorks's research through a spiritual continuum, a linear depiction of the spiritual life describing four distinct stages. Based on how people respond to the initial inventory (or survey), describing their own spiritual state, they are placed in one of four categories.

Exploring

At the time of publication, 18 percent of Episcopalians surveyed identify themselves within the first stage of spiritual growth—*exploring*. This is a particularly interesting insight given the fact that many respondents also indicate they have been attending the church longer than ten years. People in this first stage are exploring the basic beliefs expressed in the Episcopal tradition. They are drawn to the beauty of the liturgy, particularly Holy Eucharist. At the same time, they are eager for a deeper understanding of the sacraments and for help from the church in that regard. They affirm belief in God, though they are not sure what faith claims they would make about Christ. Generally speaking, faith is not a significant part of their life on a day-to-day basis.

Growing

The majority surveyed (53 percent) identify themselves within the second stage of spiritual growth—*growing*. They are committed to the Christian faith, but they still have many questions and would not speak of having a personal relationship with God in Christ. People in the first two stages of the continuum are highly dependent on the church, especially the clergy, to help them grow in faith. Such growth requires development of a relationship with God in Christ—and this can be tricky for Episcopalians, who don't always identify with language of a personal relationship with God. An authentic vision of this relationship can often be accomplished by exploration of personal spiritual practices during the week, when people are not in church. Such practices may include prayer, time in solitude, and reflection on scripture.

Deepening

Twenty-four percent of parishioners identify themselves within the third stage of spiritual growth—*deepening* their relationship with God in Christ. They describe having a personal relationship with God, and they are moving toward a place where they value that personal relationship with God even more than their particular church membership. They feel close to Christ and depend on him daily for guidance. One person described this stage as a person driving a car with God in the passenger seat, always assisting in life's navigation. For this group, opportunities to have spiritual friendships, mentors, or small-group connections are especially important, as these provide mutual accountability and moral/spiritual support.

Centered

Five percent of the respondents identify themselves within the fourth stage of spiritual growth—that of being *centered*. Of course, by no means does this stage's rank imply that the spiritual journey is over or that this group cannot enjoy further growth. But for this small percentage, a personal relationship with God in Christ is the most important relationship in their lives. Picking up the automotive analogy again, in this case, God is driving the car, and the person at this stage is in the passenger seat.

Catalysts for Spiritual Growth

The point of this continuum is to express the aspiration that people will move deeper in their own faith, that they will experience real spiritual growth, which we define as growth in love of God and love of neighbor. This linear model for spiritual growth may not *fully* explain the miracle of deepening a life with God. There are other models out there that address different aspects of the mystery of growth. But this continuum can be helpful, particularly as we focus on the movement in the continuum. The movement from one stage to the next is supported by beliefs or practices that serve as impetus for deeper engagement in life with God. Based on our research, four catalysts, in particular, make a difference.

Engagement with scripture

At every stage along the continuum, engagement with scripture is transformative. When Episcopal congregations go through the RenewalWorks process, one of the most common responses is for congregations to find a way to engage with scripture as a community.

Transforming power of the eucharist

For Episcopalians, especially for those beginning an intentional spiritual journey with God in Christ, participation in the eucharist is key. The more that churches can help people grow in understanding this mysterious sacrament, the further people move along the spiritual continuum.

Deeper prayer life

Research indicates a lack of confidence and satisfaction with prayer life. Apart from cracking open the Book of Common Prayer, many Episcopalians don't really know what a prayer life looks like. But a discernible deepening of one's relationship with God happens in the same way any relationship grows—through time spent in conversation. The more that we call people to an active prayer life, one marked by the varieties of prayer experience (confession, praise, intercession, thanksgiving, and contemplation) and by balancing listening *and* speaking, the more they will grow.

These transformations hinge in large part on the commitment of the leader to their own discipleship, including clarity of belief, dedication to spiritual practice, and service in the world. Leaders can't give what they don't have. To attend to their own spiritual health, leaders need to stay connected to the reasons they got into ministry in the first place, to remember their first love.

Indexing Spiritual Vitality

Another insight that emerged from this research is an index—that is, a number given to a congregation based on the results of the inventory. The index is made up of three components: the church's role, personal spiritual practices, and faith in action. It bears some resemblance to principles of the recovery movement, which emphasize a gathering of people, a commitment to daily engagement, working on recovery one day at a time, and service (or putting faith into action).

It's tempting to think of the index as a grade, which is not the intention at all. Rather, the index number provides a starting point, a place to measure for future growth and transformation. Perhaps the most interesting feature about the number is not how a congregation compares to others but rather how it will compare to *itself* at some future date.

This book explores the findings of the RenewalWorks surveys and ministries and offers insight into how congregations might apply those learnings to their own context. We'll begin by discussing some distinctive characteristics of Episcopal congregations, noting several archetypes that are common in the Episcopal Church. Then we'll consider the five best practice principles—the signs of life—with consideration of how each finds its foundation in scripture and liturgy.

We offer these insights in hopes for the church. As the book begins, we invite readers to join in prayer for the church, perhaps using this prayer that appears in several places in the Book of Common Prayer. It shows up in the service for the Great Vigil of Easter, in the Liturgy for Good Friday, and in the Ordination Services for Bishop and Priest.

Pray with us:

> O God of unchangeable power and eternal light: Look favorably on your whole Church, that wonderful and sacred mystery; by the effectual working of your providence, carry out in tranquility the plan of salvation; let the whole world see and know that things which were being cast down are being raised up, and things which had grown old are being made new, and that all things are being brought to their perfection by him through whom all things were made, your Son Jesus Christ our Lord; who lives and reigns with you, in the unity of the Holy Spirit, one God, for ever and ever. *Amen.*

Questions
for Reflection

As you look back on your life, have there been periods of spiritual growth? What were the catalysts that caused them?

Were there times when you felt stalled or stuck spiritually? What were the catalysts behind such experiences?

How do you react to the idea of a spiritual continuum? Do you think that spiritual growth has a linear dimension? Are there other ways of thinking about spiritual growth?

How do you react to the idea of a spiritual vitality index? Do you think that spiritual vitality can be measured? Why or why not?

1

Archetypes of the Spiritual Journey

Where is your church on the spiritual journey?

In order to make progress along this spiritual journey, it helps to know where your congregation is. As noted in the introduction's discussion of a spiritual continuum, our spiritual lives range from exploratory to a sense of centeredness. And while it's important to examine that inner spiritual life of the individual, it's equally important to get a sense of the spiritual life of the community. This requires a close look at the current state of your congregation, comprising not only the individual spiritual lives of its members but also the character of the congregation, its profile, its personality, its archetype.

Communities of all sorts have personalities—cultures they've developed over time. And while similar churches are by no means monolithic or homogeneous, we can identify some predominant characteristics among them. You might think of them as patterns or traits, and, indeed, such traits persist over generations, for good or ill. The same is true of corporations. It's true of sports teams. Lord knows, it is true of family systems. And apparently, it is true of churches.

If one doubts that this kind of characterization applies to faith communities, consider the biblical record. In several places in scripture, we can observe distinct characteristics of congregations. Perhaps this is most apparent in New Testament letters to some of the early churches. Paul's letter to the Philippians speaks of a resilient community marked by joy and faithfulness amid adversity. That is a very different account than Paul's letter to the Galatians, where he describes a church lacking clarity about its mission. This has, in turn, led to division and exclusion and triggers Paul's anger. (And one would never want to be on the receiving end of Paul's anger!) That profile is different from the church in Corinth, accustomed as it is to controversy and marked by factions fighting on all kinds of issues (issues, in fact, that the church *still* fights about!). These letters (and we suspect a few are still missing) depict a contentious place, an unsettled spirit. And then compare Corinth to the culture of the church in Ephesus, which Paul describes as a marvel and miracle of inclusion, where grace leads to a whole new way of life and dividing walls are torn down.

One can also turn to the first chapters of the Revelation to John, as the author addresses seven churches and describes the character profiles of each community. The church in Ephesus is marked by endurance, but it seems to have lost track of its first love (Revelation 2:1-7). The church in Smyrna seems to be both impoverished and rich at the same time (Revelation 2:8-11). The church in Pergamum is susceptible to teaching that pulls it away from the gospel passed on to them (Revelation 2:12-17). And so it continues, with portraits of distinct communities addressed with both praise and criticism, offering a realistic and rigorous assessment of their current state and instructions about different ways for them to move forward.

RenewalWorks seeks to follow these scriptural examples in naming and assessing the current state of the congregation and then providing insight for ways to deepen and grow. The ministry asks the questions: What spiritual characteristics can we identify in congregations today? What are the strengths and the challenges they bear? How can communities move forward from the place in which they presently find themselves? In a season when mainline congregations, especially Episcopal churches, grapple with decline, fights within, and fears without, where can we find signs of life?

The first step is to evaluate the distinct character of each community. Speaking the truth in love, we can take a clear and courageous look at where these communities are right now. Cally Parkinson, a former senior staff member at Willow Creek church, has been a part of the spiritual assessment process for many years. She consults regularly with congregations about the research done through the REVEAL process, a spiritual assessment tool to explore spiritual vitality that provided the basic framework for the RenewalWorks inventory. In the course of her work, she came to identify eight archetypes of churches. Think of these as patterns, segments, clusters, or personalities. Parkinson describes these eight archetypes in her book, *Rise: Bold Strategies to Transform Your Church*.

Vibrant: Faith among congregants is strong and mature but still growing. People love the church.

Troubled: People are spiritually immature and unhappy with the church and with its senior pastor.

Complacent: Faith is surprisingly underdeveloped, given that attenders are longtime churchgoers.

Introverted: Faith is strong, but faith-based behaviors are lacking.

Average: No spiritual measures deviate from the norm.

Extroverted: Faith is underdeveloped, but community service is embraced.

Self-motivated: Faith is strong across the board, yet people are un-enthused about the church.

Energized: Faith is somewhat underdeveloped but growing, and people love the church.

While many of the congregations studied by Parkinson and evaluated in the REVEAL process differ from Episcopal communities, the research still offers quite a few lessons for Episcopalians. Based on research in more than 300 Episcopal congregations, RenewalWorks has gained significant insight into how these archetypes might apply to the Episcopal world. Notably, the Episcopal congregations engaged with this research fall into *three* of these eight categories: troubled, complacent, and extroverted.

Let us consider these three particular archetypes more closely, looking at what they have to say about the current state of these types of congregations—and what congregations of such character might do to move forward. See if you recognize your congregation in any of these profiles.

❖ The Troubled Church
Rooted, Restless, and Ready to Grow

Rooted and restless. That's how former Archbishop George Carey described one congregation he visited. We may be familiar with churches that are primarily *rooted*. There's some truth to the description of Anglicans as the "frozen chosen." For those churches, the words that haunt any church leader come to mind: "We've never done it that way" or its corollary "We've always done it this way."

One of the great gifts of Anglicanism is its deep roots in tradition. But there is a difference between being rooted in the community of saints and being stuck in habits that have encrusted our spiritual lives. As we will see, rootedness can easily manifest itself in complacency, with no aspiration for growth or movement or transformation. That can make it difficult to think about how—or even why—the church should grow.

About half of our churches fall into this category, an archetype described as *troubled*. This description, however, calls for some explanation. By calling such churches "troubled," we are not hinting at church fights nor is it a reference to financial difficulties or scandals among the leadership. Rather, the troubledness here connotes spiritual restlessness, a sense of wanting more. Saint Augustine famously called attention to such troubledness in the opening lines of his *Confessions*: "You have made us and drawn us to yourself, and our heart is restless until it rests in you." On the one hand, such restlessness is a good thing, indicating to us that we are not where we should be. On the other hand, however, this restlessness requires guidance and initiative to begin to move.

Those in troubled churches are not exactly sure how to grow spiritually nor are they convinced that their leadership is willing or even able to help address that need. It's entirely possible the leadership doesn't really know how to help in this situation. It may not be something they were taught in seminary. In addition, those in leadership may be spiritually restless, hungry, or troubled in their own lives.

This church profile corroborates studies that indicate a spiritual restlessness in the broader culture. This restlessness has manifested in a significant increase in the number of "nones and dones" in our culture. (Nones are those who indicate no religious affiliation, the fastest growing religious identification in our culture. Dones represent those who have left the church, for any variety of reasons.) Add to that the recent experience of social distancing triggered by the COVID-19 pandemic, and we cannot deny the pervasiveness of restlessness. This collective experience, from which no one remains unaffected, has caused people to take a fresh look at what it means to be church and how they wish to affiliate with religious institutions in the days ahead (or not). Meanwhile, the church often spends time answering questions that no one is asking, leaving widespread hunger for deeper and more meaningful spiritual lives unaddressed and causing people to look elsewhere for answers.

Troubled churches have two defining characteristics. First, there is *dissatisfaction with the church and with the senior leadership* (specifically, the rector or priest-in-charge). That dissatisfaction is not a matter of disliking the person. It is not a specific argument on a theological or political point. Rather, the dissatisfaction seems to be more about a sense that the leadership has failed to provide a pathway to spiritual growth. It's a sense that there is more, but congregants flounder, not knowing what they don't know and uncertain how to move forward.

Second, the church in this archetype has a high percentage of congregants who fall into the early stages of spiritual growth (as discussed in the introduction). As such, they may show signs of spiritual apathy or stasis. Interestingly, the RenewalWorks research offers an unexpected insight: in many cases, people who have been around the church for a long time are still in a place of spiritual immaturity. For this group, participation and presence in worship hasn't led to spiritual growth—nor has activity in church programs, however frequent. People in troubled congregations depend heavily on the church leaders for spiritual traction.

So, what can be done? There is an incredible opportunity here. We can take comfort in the teachings of Jesus, especially the first beatitude, the opening line of the Sermon on the Mount: "Blessed are the poor in spirit" (Matthew 5:3). Some paraphrased versions render the verse to speak of need rather than poverty: Blessed are those *who know their need* of God. Congregants in troubled congregations are primed for more. Three practices can help congregations in the troubled archetype to get moving along the spiritual continuum.

1. Focus on the heart of the leader

I often tell those in church leadership: "You can't give what you don't have." By this, I mean that those who lead the church must focus on the authenticity of their own spiritual journey. Are they being fed? Are they being challenged? Are they still learning? Are they stuck? Or, to use an automotive metaphor, have they run out of gas, gotten a flat tire, or slipped into a ditch? Have they given up?

Clergy often feel isolated, depleted by incessant criticism and demands, and concerned about family and finances. Understandably, these issues can lead to ineffective ministry. In the next chapter, we'll focus on the role of the leader, so we'll only address this briefly here. But for movement of a community out of troubled restlessness, its leaders are called to focus on their own spiritual state. Is their own love for God and neighbor growing? Does it serve as model and inspiration for a congregation that is stuck?

2. Focus on the intersection of beliefs and practices

A journalist trying to understand the decline of mainline congregations traveled around the country to interview various churchgoers. When he asked a youth group member in the Midwest about why she was part of the church, she responded: "I love being Episcopalian. You don't have to believe anything." There's a graceful dimension to this, for sure. This young woman felt accepted in the community. But there's also a challenge that may be a serious threat to our congregations.

In Chapter 3, we explore some of these basic questions: What does it mean to be part of the community? What do we stand for? Where do we give our hearts (which is one way to think about belief)? For many congregants in troubled churches, there is a hunger for teaching about both the meaning and relevance of scripture and the liturgy, especially the sacraments. Episcopalians often don't want to be presented with a list of dogmatic demands requiring their signature. At the same time, there is a desire to know why we do what we do. As Saint Anselm put it in the latter years of the eleventh century, faith seeks understanding. Are our churches providing that?

3. Offer an integrated, high-profile, Bible-based initiative

Again and again, we see that congregations that read and study the scriptures together undergo a collective spiritual movement. That's why we've identified "Embedding Scripture in Everything" as one of the best practice principles. Chapter 4 discusses how this embedding work can be done. Wherever people are, it seems that the scripture has power to transform, regardless of how it is interpreted. We have found that if a congregation can engage in reading scripture together, perhaps over the course of a liturgical season, an academic year, or even over the course of several years, the sacred text brings people together and helps their community move forward. It's a powerful opportunity for parishioners across generations to explore the basis of their faith in age-appropriate ways. And there's significant potential for growth when congregants affirm that they can do this together.

❖ The Complacent Church
We're Fine, Thanks

In the final book of the New Testament, the author is instructed in his vision to write to one church in particular, "You are neither cold nor hot. I wish that you were either cold or hot. So, because you are lukewarm, and neither cold nor hot, I am about to spit you out of my mouth" (Revelation 3:15b-16). Harsh words for what we are calling here the "complacent church."

What does a complacent church look like? At one of the congregations involved in RenewalWorks ministry, the rector recognized that complacency aptly described his congregation, much to his chagrin. But taking a lighthearted approach, he announced that his church would be changing its tagline to: "We're spiritually shallow, and we're fine with that!" Unfortunately, this can be said of many Episcopal churches. According to our research, complacent churches represent 23 percent of our congregations.

Archetypes of the Spiritual Journey

That rector's tongue-in-cheek response indicates a deeper challenge. In many churches—and congregants—there is no expectation of transformation or spiritual growth. And in many complacent churches, talk of spiritual growth can be (at least, initially) met with resistance. In one congregation, the rector had her own conversion experience, realizing that if the church was not about spiritual growth, there was no point in meeting. She began to speak incessantly about the call to this kind of growth. With singular focus, she preached, taught, and wrote about this need. When it came time for gathering annual pledges to support the ministry of the church, members of the congregation reached out by phone and personal visits in an organized campaign to get financial commitments for the coming year. In one of these calls, the person being asked for a pledge replied: "I don't understand all this talk about spiritual growth. I want to know at what vestry meeting it was decided that we are about spiritual growth. I want to see the resolution."

Indeed, spiritual growth is not a universal expectation. If a congregation wishes to establish spiritual growth as a priority, it will call for conversation, education, and consensus that spiritual growth is an important value. Such a commitment brings change. It's a call to transformation, and we all know how much we like change. As that patron saint of organizational management, Dilbert, once said: "Change is good. You go first."

There are two defining characteristics of a complacent church. First, there is spiritual apathy. Congregants demonstrate little interest in or commitment to growing their faith, especially to developing their faith beyond the hour or so they grant the church on a Sunday morning. This frame of mind can be attributed to several factors. Some in our culture admit that they are simply too busy to think about the spiritual life. Others have been wounded by organized religion. Others have given spiritual growth a try in the past and have come to expect that nothing could ever change. Second, like those in troubled churches, congregants may have attended church for years, yet they still seem to find themselves in the earliest stages of spiritual maturity. Long tenure in a church does not mean that there has been any spiritual growth.

As noted in the introduction, it's worth paying attention to the reasons why people—especially those in the Episcopal Church—choose to go to church. Some attend primarily for the social aspect. Others are drawn to the aesthetics of a particular church. They find the music or architecture to be pleasing, perhaps even inspiring. Others come because the church is an avenue for service in the world. Others come because it is simply what they have always done. Perhaps they attend to please a family member, a spouse, or a parent, which can be an act of kind generosity but is rarely an avenue for spiritual growth. These are each and all noble aspirations, and they are good reasons to gather. But they don't necessarily correspond to a desire for spiritual growth, which as Chapter 1 described, has to do with growing in love of God and neighbor. These are satisfied with the church as it is, which can complicate the path to spiritual growth. But naming the issue and challenging folks to a different way of viewing their spiritual lives can provide forward movement on the spiritual continuum.

One church grappled with this dynamic. Brenda Husson, rector, and Ryan Fleenor, vicar, wrote about the experience of their congregation, St. James' Church on Madison Avenue in New York City. The article, "When Fine Isn't Enough," is reprinted in the appendix, but consider the following highlight of that piece:

> Whenever parishioners were asked what they loved about St. James', they always spoke first about the sense of community they found here. It's hard to complain about that, but there was no talk of transformation or God, let alone Jesus. And stewardship (again, fine by the standards of many parishes) was flat, indicating that we were, for many of our parishioners, just another nonprofit. Maybe their favorite, but not a place that was changing or challenging them at the center of their lives.

As we asked in the introduction: Is flat the new "up" in the Episcopal Church, as many clergy have come to believe with some sense of resignation? What steps can a complacent church take?

1. Focus on the heart of the leader

Transforming complacent churches requires leaders and congregants to raise their expectations on spiritual growth. One clergyperson spoke with her congregation about the need for spiritual growth in the community and in the individual lives of congregations. She framed it in terms of a call to transformation, and one of her congregants responded: "I don't know why you are talking about transformation. I don't expect anything to happen to me when I come to church." In other words, there was no expectation of any change whatsoever. As we've noted, that may be a result of failed efforts in the past. Maybe there were wounds at the hand of institutional religion. Maybe that was out of fear, but a pathway out of complacency calls for an expectation of movement, that there will be a difference made. Such initiative requires leadership with a heart inclined toward spiritual journeying. Clergy, for instance, are called to preach and teach consistently and authentically about the importance of spiritual growth.

2. Explore small groups

One way to bring change comes by welcoming people into smaller groups where they can tell their own stories and safely converse about their own spiritual journeys. Episcopal polity focuses on our gatherings for worship, such that God is worshipped with glorious liturgy and beautiful music. But it is possible to attend church for decades, sit in the same pew, and yet never know the names of those sitting around us, let alone know their stories. Those gathering for worship can be enriched by other kinds of gatherings throughout the week, where people are known and can come to know others.

Some of those small groups already exist in almost every church (choirs, altar guilds, church committees). These can be transformed in simple ways. The mere introduction of prayer or reflection on scripture can transform a task-oriented committee into a spiritual community. One church had a choir with members who had been singing together for decades. In all those years, they had never stopped rehearsing to have a conversation about what their ministry of music meant to them, how they saw God in that offering, and how it had changed them.

A commitment to regular conversation about God's activity in our lives can enliven existing ministries. An occasional conversation about why engagement with a particular ministry is spiritually meaningful can knit the community together. Book groups, prayer groups, and Bible studies all vary in the ways they help people move forward spiritually. If they become places where the text is studied in a way that applies to the lives of participants—that is, if what we call the "so-what factor" is being explored, transformation can happen.

❖ The Extroverted Church
Kind of Like the Rotary Club

Thank God for the Rotary Club—and the many organizations that offer remarkable service to communities around the globe. But it is worth asking whether there is something distinctive about the church in its ministry in the world—or are we simply another well-meaning nonprofit. Our research indicates that relative to other denominations, those in the Episcopal Church have a deep commitment to mission and outreach. Presiding Bishop Michael Curry has spoken about the remarkable increase in the outward focus of the church. When he was ordained more than thirty years ago, few churches had robust outreach programs. Now, he rarely finds a parish that does not have that kind of ministry. While our hearts are gladdened by this embrace of outreach, it also raises the question posed in the introduction: does more church activity necessarily mean more spiritual growth? Our research says it does not.

About 25 percent of Episcopal congregations can be described as extroverted. That means their common life is characterized by a deep commitment to service in the community, reaching beyond the walls of the church. This outward focus is clearly mandated by scripture, perhaps most notably in an apocalyptic saying of Jesus in Matthew 25.

"When the Son of Man comes in his glory," Jesus proclaims, those who have ministered to the poor, the hungry, the naked, the imprisoned will learn that they were really serving him.

The Letter of James also addresses the intersection of faith and works: "What good is it, my brothers and sisters, if you say you have faith but do not have works? Can faith save you? If a brother or sister is naked and lacks daily food, and one of you says to them, 'Go in peace; keep warm and eat your fill,' and yet you do not supply their bodily needs, what is the good of that? So faith by itself, if it has no works, is dead" (James 2:14-17). The writer observes that in this first-century congregation, an affirmation of faith existed apart from faith in action. What we find in Episcopal culture these days is a bit different. It is often the case that acts of service are key, but they lack an anchor in belief. They are indeed, as Mother Teresa said, a matter of doing "something beautiful for God," but there is lack of clarity about their rootedness in faith.

Scripture can provide that anchor. So can the liturgy of the church. It's been said that the most important part of the service of the Holy Eucharist is the dismissal, where people who have received spiritual nourishment are sent out into the world. We say: "Go in peace to love and serve the Lord." Some churches even have a sign over the exit that reads: "The worship is over. The service begins."

The promises made at baptism stress this outward focus. They call the community to proclaim by word and example the good news of God in Christ. They challenge the community to seek and serve Christ in all persons. They ask the community to strive for justice and peace, respecting the dignity of every human being. These promises, renewed every time there is a baptism, offer a wonderful integration of faith and service, providing warrant for an outward focus.

So, what steps toward spiritual growth can the extroverted church take?

1. Pastor the community

This best practice principle is a key transformative element for extroverted churches. Pastoring the community means integrating worship, prayer, and scripture reflection in ministry efforts. For instance, if a church has a soup kitchen, volunteers can gather to offer a prayer for those whom they are serving. If a church has a thrift shop or a food pantry, volunteers can gather for a moment of biblical reflection. One large and thriving thrift shop had morning and afternoon shifts, so they decided to schedule a fifteen-minute overlap to ask the morning volunteers where they had seen God at work over the past few hours and to ask the afternoon volunteers about their hopes for the afternoon. This was then followed by prayer together, a recognition that their work was God's work in the world.

These simple steps have no budgetary, staffing, or programmatic implications. But they can transform an outreach effort and clarify why the church is involved in such work, which results in stronger sustenance of that ministry. And they can lead to a deeper discussion about the ways that the God of our tradition is connected to the brokenness of this world.

2. Focus on the intersection of beliefs and practices

Along those same lines, extroverted congregations can grow as they offer teaching and reflection, considering why we serve and how that kind of activity grows out of our beliefs. This process can unfold in preaching and teaching and other forms of communication. Clergy can offer Bible studies and other forums that specifically point to scriptures about belief in a God who hears the suffering of God's people, to a lord and savior who came not to be served but to serve, to a Holy Spirit that anoints to bring liberty to the oppressed (Luke 4:18). The church calendar is filled with the lives of saints, ancient and contemporary, who demonstrate how their deep belief moved them to service. As noted, baptism contains promises that call us to strive for justice and peace and respect the dignity of all persons, to seek and serve Christ in all persons.

Witnessing and testimonials may seem foreign to many Episcopalians but offering opportunities for members of the congregation to talk about how their beliefs inform their commitment to service can effect real transformation throughout the community.

Also consider anchoring such service in particular scripture passages, in the liturgy (as praying shapes our believing), and in theological reflection. Perhaps offer a short course on the scriptural mandate to be of service. Explore the witness of the prophets. Tell the story of the exodus, how God responded to the people's suffering. Hear what Jesus has to say about ministry to the least in the kingdom, visiting the lonely, feeding the hungry, healing the sick, freeing the prisoner (his inaugural sermon in Luke 4, for instance). Do a deep dive into the scripture to learn how service runs as a theme throughout scripture, especially as Jesus describes himself as the one who came to serve, not to be served.

3. Create a sense of ownership

Spiritual role models play an important part in creating a sense of ownership and spiritual growth. The leader, as one of the key spiritual role models, should set a personal example of discipleship and invite other congregational leaders to follow suit. Congregational leaders, clergy and lay, should be involved in service—and in connecting that service to scripture. Humble and transparent communication can be transformative. Martin Luther King Jr. offered an example of this type of public profession of faith and service. When he was organizing groups to stand up for civil rights in the south, he asked participants to include daily scripture reading and prayer, an outward and visible sign that these beliefs were integral to the success of the movement.

GETTING READY TO MOVE

These three archetypes—troubled, complacent, and extroverted—offer a sense of where many Episcopal congregations find themselves these days. It's a challenging set of images, for sure, but not a hopeless one.

The research that informs this work discovered some churches that exhibited a distinctive spiritual vitality. Researchers gathered this small sampling of congregations to see what was going on. They found several common themes, activities, and approaches. They shared similarities in cultures even though the congregations ranged widely in character—some were rural, some more urban. Some were large, some small. Out of conversation with these churches, five best practice principles emerged:

- Focus on the Heart of the Leader
- Get People Moving
- Embed Scripture in Everything
- Create a Sense of Ownership
- Pastor the Community

These five best practice principles present Episcopal congregations with a roadmap for moving forward. There *are* signs of life. Our God is a God of hope.

Questions
for Reflection

What do you make of the idea that congregations have personalities? Does the idea of church archetypes resonate with you?

Do you recognize your congregation in any of these archetypes?

What might you do if you were interested in making a shift in your church's archetype?

2

The Heart of the Leader

A church was looking for a new rector. The search committee narrowed its field of candidates and met for extensive interviews with a few prospective leaders. The chair of the committee planned to ask each candidate to begin the interview with devotional time, offering a prayer and leading a reflection on scripture. One candidate thanked the chair and shared the story of interaction with another search committee. When the candidate was about to begin an interview with that other group, the candidate asked if they would like to begin with a prayer. The chair of that committee responded: "We don't really do that."

Another person consulting with congregations about spiritual vitality was holding a conference call with a rector and several lay leaders of the church. As the conversation began, this consultant (a layperson) invited the rector to begin the time together with a prayer. The rector responded: "I'm not really comfortable doing that."

Compare these scenarios to the practice of a rector who comes to church extra early on Sundays. Of course, clergy generally arrive with time to prepare for Sunday worship. One must ensure the altar is set, the doors are open, the heat or air conditioning hasn't gone out, and bulletins are ready (despite lingering typos). A rector often does all that, allotting an hour or so for such preparatory work. But this rector shows up even an hour earlier, spending an hour praying for the gatherings that morning. Early on a Sunday morning, one can find that rector standing in the narthex, praying for the ministry of the ushers, or climbing stairs to the choir loft to pray for those offering the ministry of music, or moving to the sacristy in prayer for the altar guild.

These actions reveal a lot about the heart of a leader. They express a conviction that both the leader and the congregation are dependent on God's help in whatever they do. They reveal a heart for all the people who come together to make Sunday possible.

The truth is that leaders of congregations vary in the ways they practice their spiritual leadership. Some are more effective than others. Some are more committed to this kind of leadership than others. Of course, there is nothing new about this. In the 1930s, Evelyn Underhill wrote to the Archbishop of Canterbury, Cosmo Gordon Lang, sharing her observations of the clergy of her day. An excerpt from this letter indicates that she detected growth opportunities for the clergy (the full letter can be found in the appendix). She wrote:

> May it please your Grace: I desire very humbly to suggest with bishops assembled at Lambeth that the greatest and most necessary work they could do at the present time for the renewal of the Anglican Church would be to call the clergy as a whole, solemnly and insistently to a greater interiority and cultivation of the personal life of prayer.... The real hunger among laity is not for halting attempts to reconcile theology and physical science but for the deep things of the Spirit....We look to the clergy to help and direct our spiritual growth.
>
> God is the interesting thing about religion, and people are hungry for God.

What was it about the state of the Church of England in those days that compelled her to write this letter? Why did she need to remind the Archbishop of Canterbury that God is the interesting thing about religion and that people are hungry for God? Shouldn't that be standard with clergy? Her letter raises the question before us today about how clergy can be called to a greater cultivation of a personal life of prayer and devotion. This is the subject of the present chapter, as we come to the first and central best practice principle for spiritually vital congregations: *the heart of the leader.*

Dwight Zscheile, professor at Luther Seminary in Minnesota, a well-known expert on spiritual growth, cites a survey of Presbyterian ministers in which 85 percent said they had no personal practice of prayer or reflection on scripture apart from their Sunday worship preparations. It's no wonder congregations are left hungering for God. The fact is many clergy may be hungering for God themselves. For that reason, nurturing the heart of the leader matters. And for that reason, it is the first of the five best practice principles that we will consider. The other four depend on it.

Research indicates many growth opportunities for clergy as they shepherd congregations. Currently, 42 percent of Episcopal respondents have never met with members of the clergy staff individually to discuss spiritual matters. Almost half of the respondents have never talked with a spiritual mentor of any kind. One might imagine that many clergy leaders eagerly desire this kind of connection and spiritual mentorship. For many, this is why they became ordained in the first place. Spiritual mentorship is often their first love. Yet, for far too many, that love falls to the wayside, neglected and even forgotten.

Not only is this detrimental to their own spiritual growth but also it contributes to the overall decline of spiritual health within a congregation. As discussed earlier in the spiritual continuum, almost two-thirds of Episcopalians indicate they are in the first two stages of spiritual growth (exploring and growing). That is true even for some people with long tenure in the church. For that large group of Episcopalians, the role of the church and especially clergy in guiding them is essential. Many people hunger for a deeper spiritual life, a deeper relationship with God, and they simply don't know how to go about developing that relationship. Many have no idea how to get started reading the Bible. One parishioner told the rector he was reading the Bible from start to finish. He never made it past Leviticus. Many have no idea how to develop a prayer life. They pray on Sundays during worship—or when there's a crisis of some sort—but they don't know how to establish a routine of daily prayer.

Congregants look to the clergy, especially the rector or senior pastor, to guide them. They need a teacher who will motivate, teach, and inspire them in reading scripture. Just as Jesus taught his disciples to pray, giving them the Lord's Prayer, spiritual leaders today must respond to the desire for an authentic prayer life, providing instruction and modeling a prayer life themselves. For long-tenured and spiritually young parishioners alike, the clergy's ability to make these ancient practices come to life and pertain to life is essential for congregations to thrive.

In addition, an ability to teach and focus on basic Episcopal beliefs and practices matters a great deal. Our research shows that growing in understanding of the eucharist, baptism, and the creeds are important catalysts for spiritual growth. It's been interesting to observe how the transformative power of the eucharist, coupled with deeper understanding of its mysteries, can change lives. This behooves clergy to be teachers, exploring basic Episcopal beliefs, both in the context of worship (e.g., an instructed eucharist offered on a regular basis) and outside the Sunday service (e.g., in church classes or individual mentoring). Numerous resources are available to help clergy provide this kind of help—from books to videos, Zoom Bible studies and online Christian formation. These programs do not have to be reinvented in every parish; the leader simply has to offer and encourage people to take part, using resources available in the wider church.

Currently, this desire for teaching and formation is not being met in many congregations. Respondents consistently report a gap between their desire for guidance in spiritual practices and their satisfaction with the way their church supports those practices. Engagement in scripture ranks as one of the top needs—and biggest disappointments. This finding provides leaders with a challenging opportunity: how can leaders invite parishioners to engage with scripture in new and interesting ways?

At the same time, clergy (especially rectors, priests-in-charge, and vicars) increasingly report that the stressful reality of their jobs often pulls them away from a ministry focused on spiritual growth. They have been removed from the reason they pursued ordination in the first place, away from their "first love." In the face of such challenges, clergy must find ways to focus on their own spiritual practices and further their own spiritual journey. Wardens and vestry members can support clergy in this process, allowing time, space, and financial resources for ongoing spiritual development, which in turn allows clergy to return to a leadership role that models discipleship and spiritual sustainability.

Such spiritual development and nurture of clergy may be the most important factor in the spiritual growth of congregants. Clergy can't give what they don't have. And that leads us to ask specifically about the qualities of spiritual leaders.

❖ What Are the Characteristics of Spiritual Leaders?

In the work that led to RenewalWorks, leaders of sixteen especially vital congregations met with researchers. They explored the heart of the leader and agreed on four characteristics of leaders of congregations that exhibit this kind of distinctive vitality:

Spiritual leaders exhibit a deep personal humility and an intense professional will

In his book, *Good to Great,* Jim Collins notes that the effective leader combines these two qualities of humility and will. That is, these types of leaders can get things done, but they refrain from putting themselves front and center in every situation.

Perhaps the greatest model of this kind of leadership in the Old Testament is Moses. He is depicted as being far from perfect, but he also exhibited both humility and devoted willpower. Scripture describes Moses as meek, as evidenced by his self-doubt and reluctance to serve as God instructs him. At times, it seems that Moses felt like his call was a wrong number (Exodus 4:10-13). Yet, as Moses led the children of Israel through the wilderness, with many distractions, numerous crises, constant complaint, and persistent criticism, he kept his eyes on the prize, demonstrating that intense personal will. (It is no wonder, then, that his leadership became frequent inspiration for leaders of the Civil Rights Movement.)

Saint Paul also emerges as a single-minded biblical leader who exhibited humility. Readers of the New Testament may not readily identify him as humble, but he often described his own shortcomings and the mistakes he had made in life. As he wrote to early churches, he was aware of his own limits. Yet at the same time, if one were ever to look for a spiritual leader with intense professional will, Paul would fill the bill.

Spiritual leaders work on their own discipleship

Second, an effective leader must be working on their own discipleship. In the same way that congregations are only as spiritually healthy and vital as the members of those congregations, so the leader's heart is key to that vitality. Leaders make disciples by becoming disciples themselves. By discipleship, we mean a commitment to be a follower of Jesus: to embrace his teachings, to work for the healing of the world, and to take on the role of a servant.

In his Great Commission to the disciples at the end of the Gospel of Matthew (28:16-20), Jesus sends the disciples out with this task: go and make disciples. For many in the Episcopal culture, this call can seem foreign or even off-putting. That is especially true for those who have made their way to the Episcopal Church as a refugee, after having been wounded by proselytizing, overbearing, and dogmatically rigid Christians. How can leaders practice discipleship in ways that are loving, life-giving, and liberating, to borrow a phrase from Presiding Bishop Curry? This is one of the great challenges currently facing spiritual leaders.

Spiritual leaders model discipleship

Leaders of congregations are to be models of discipleship themselves. It's been said that one of the terms for spiritual leader is parson, a term that comes from the word person. That term suggests that the leader of a congregation shows what it means to be a person of faith, a spiritual person, one who is following Jesus. In the Book of Common Prayer, the Outline of the Faith talks about the ministry of all persons, and particularly leaders. For all the ministers of the church—laypersons, deacons, priests, and bishops—the call is to represent Christ. For many spiritual leaders, that calls for a sense of vulnerability and transparency. (For more on the importance of the theme of vulnerability, consider the work of Brené Brown, who speaks powerfully about the need for this attribute to be in evidence among leaders.)

The New Testament record indicates this truth. With plenty of examples of transparency, we read about the foibles of the disciples, especially Peter. It would have been easy to eliminate all the stories that showed the flaws of Peter and his colleagues. But these pillars of the early church, who turned the world upside down in short order, all had their shortcomings. Scripture records their missteps, now on full display for all of history to witness.

Spiritual leaders focus on growing hearts

Spiritual leaders focus primarily on growing hearts, not growing attendance or budgets or buildings. Growing according to those metrics may come, to be sure. But the primary call is to be single-minded about forming disciples. Everything the church does should be seen through the lens of how it contributes to spiritual growth—that is, how people can grow in love of God and neighbor. This kind of non-anxious, hopeful ministry may indeed call for a leap of faith. It can be hard when the spiritual leader must focus on paying staff and keeping the lights on. But this focus is key to spiritual vitality.

One way to focus on growing hearts is to ask a series of questions about every ministry in a congregation. This can be done by the leadership reviewing all ministries or by leaders in each ministry engaging in their own separate discussion. This evaluation should include such questions as:

1. *What do we do?* It's amazing how many ministries in the church go on year after year without any reflection on what the ministry is about. It may also be fruitful to discuss what the ministry is *not* about. What are the limits of the tasks that those involved will take on?

2. *Why do we do it?* Is the ministry continued simply because it's been done before? Is there warrant in scripture or tradition for the work we are doing? Is the ministry addressing a need or has it outlived its usefulness? That is, how does what we do as a church differ from the very good work done by other nonprofit organizations?

3. *How does this ministry contribute to spiritual growth?* This may be the most important question for congregations. Often "mission creep" means that congregations engage in activities that are not really geared to help people grow spiritually. This can happen for all kinds of reasons. Perhaps a parishioner has a favorite program, a pet project in mind. Perhaps the congregation has never clearly committed to spiritual growth. Perhaps there is no understanding of how to go about deepening spiritual growth. Vitality seems to follow this kind of singular focus— and complacency seems to follow without such focus.

4. *What do we want to do moving forward?* How can all the activities and ministries of the church be reoriented toward spiritual growth? We find that such reorientation is often more about

culture than program and doesn't require new staff or a new line item in the budget. It may simply mean thinking in new ways about what we are already doing, inviting God's power and presence into the existing, even longstanding, ministry.

To entertain these kinds of questions takes leadership and perhaps courage. It can be difficult, even deemed unkind, to change the character of ministries, let alone bring change to a congregational culture. But it is part of the hard work of leadership, making spiritual growth the priority in congregations. It is about gaining clarity of vision.

❖ How Do We Think About the Leadership Role of Clergy?

The key characteristics of spiritual leaders should be part of our discussion about how clergy leadership is regarded in our churches. How is that role of leader understood in light of scripture? How is it understood throughout our Anglican tradition? How is it understood in light of our culture?

To begin, we look to scripture (practicing the best practice principle of embedding scripture in everything, which we'll explore in greater depth in Chapter 4). We've already discussed Moses as a remarkable spiritual leader in the Old Testament. Fast-forwarding to the first century, as the church gets off the ground, we see the gospels sharing a vision of Jesus as spiritual leader. Jesus articulates certain expectations for his followers: that they should love God and love neighbor as self (again, that's how we have come to understand spiritual growth). When his disciples jockey for political position, imagining who will be chief of staff in the kingdom of God, who will get the corner office, Jesus speaks of the greatness that comes with service: "Whoever wishes to become great among you must be your servant" (Mark 10:43b).

Saint Paul, as he guides the first congregations of the Jesus Movement, also provides a vision of spiritual leadership. He describes himself as a servant of God and steward of the mysteries. That doesn't mean he is in charge. That doesn't mean he knows everything. It does mean he is called to a ministry of service, a theme picked up in the famous Prayer of Saint Francis, who asked for the grace to be made an instrument of God's peace (Book of Common Prayer, p. 833).

As we think about leaders in a congregation, it's helpful to consider the commissioning that comes in the Liturgy for the Ordination of a Priest in the Book of Common Prayer, starting on page 531. In the course of that service, the bishop gives the charge to the person to be ordained, providing a job description of sorts:

> As a priest, it will be your task to proclaim by word and deed the Gospel of Jesus Christ, and to fashion your life in accordance with its precepts. You are to love and serve the people among whom you work, caring alike for young and old, strong and weak, rich and poor. You are to preach, to declare God's forgiveness to penitent sinners, to pronounce God's blessing, to share in the administration of Holy Baptism and in the celebration of the mysteries of Christ's Body and Blood, and to perform the other ministrations entrusted to you. In all that you do, you are to nourish Christ's people from the riches of his grace, and strengthen them to glorify God in this life and in the life to come.

Embedded in this charge are many of the principles we've already discussed. The leader is to proclaim the good news of the Jesus Movement by word and deed, to be a preacher, a teacher, and a communicator to a community that needs to hear that word. The leader is to model discipleship, fashioning life in accordance with precepts of the Christian faith. How often have you heard of a congregant who left the church because of disappointment with the behavior of the clergy, indiscretions about money or sex, or poor treatment of parishioners or employees? The leader is to be a servant, carrying out a variety of sacramental tasks as outward signs of God's grace, leading to perhaps the most important charge in the ordination service: to nourish God's people from the riches of God's grace. This powerful statement recognizes the deep hunger for spiritual life. And it says that those needs will be met, that the God-shaped space in each person will be fulfilled through the riches of God's grace. This will not happen because of the wisdom or competence or charisma or magnificence of the leader. It will happen because God's grace is at work.

The Book of Common Prayer offers additional insight in the Liturgy for the Celebration of a New Ministry, a service where a new rector is installed as leader of the congregation. As with many of our liturgies, it's helpful to look at the prayers in the service to figure out what the service is all about. With that in mind, consider this prayer (found on pages 562-563) offered by the new rector, the new spiritual leader of a congregation:

> O Lord my God, I am not worthy to have you come under my roof; yet you have called your servant to stand in your house, and to serve at your altar. To you and to your service I devote myself, body, soul, and spirit. Fill my memory with the record of your mighty works; enlighten my understanding with the light of your Holy Spirit; and may all the desires of my heart and will center in what you would have me do. Make me an instrument of your salvation for the people entrusted to my care, and grant that I may faithfully administer your holy Sacraments, and by my life and teaching set forth your true and living Word. Be always with me in carrying out the duties of my ministry. In prayer, quicken my devotion; in praises, heighten my love and gratitude; in preaching, give me readiness of thought and expression; and grant that, by the clearness and brightness of your holy Word, all the world may be drawn into your blessed kingdom. All this I ask for the sake of your Son our Savior Jesus Christ. *Amen.*

Again, this prayer reflects themes we have already discussed. It calls on the leader to serve in a spirit of humility, echoing the words of a Roman centurion, a leader in the community who approached Jesus with a need for healing (Matthew 8:5-13). The prayer suggests that the new rector will seek to be filled with the memory of God's deeds and share them. The new leader will be a teacher, preacher, and communicator. And that person will serve as a model, as an instrument of God's salvation, not for the sake of personal aggrandizement but for the sake of God's blessed kingdom, the beloved community.

One of the challenges many congregations face is the temptation to look to models of spiritual leadership found neither in scripture nor tradition but those offered by contemporary culture, by "kingdoms of this world." One rector of a large, complicated parish regularly reminds his staff of the derivation of the word: rector. He claims, perhaps tongue-in-cheek, that the word comes from rex, the Latin word for king. That rector's humor aside, it often appears that some leaders sincerely believe this about their role: *I'm king. Listen to me.* For too many people, this is the only way they know how to be a leader.

Similarly, many congregations subscribe to the notion that the model for a spiritual leader comes from the corporate world. Of course, congregations do often function as small—or even not-so-small—businesses. Skills in finance, technology, and human resources can all be significant instruments of ministry. Yet again, as we speak of spiritual leadership, we must ask how leadership in a faith community, specifically a Christian community, differs from other organizations.

Spiritual leaders often focus on aspects of their vocation that may be essential but not primary. For instance, some clergy see themselves as teachers. Some as preachers. Some as activists for social justice. Some as managers. Some as pastors. All of these matter a great deal, to be sure, but the premise of this book is that spiritual leaders should be primarily focused on spiritual growth. Consider the following two models of such leadership.

Spiritual coaches

First, spiritual leaders may serve as *spiritual coaches*. We have in our culture all kinds of coaches: nutrition coaches, executive coaches, financial coaches, yoga instructors, fitness trainers, and so on. And all of these roles focus, in one way or another, on transformation. For too long in the Episcopal culture, however, there has been no focus on change, growth, challenge, or transformation. As noted earlier, many of our churches could be described as complacent. A spiritual coach, then, works with individuals and congregations to heighten a sense of possibility, to challenge and encourage, to open pathways for the amazingly graceful work that God wishes to do in us and among us and through us. We'll talk more about that when we consider the best practice principle of getting people moving.

Doyt Conn serves as the rector of Seattle's Church of the Epiphany, a congregation in a part of the world that is often described as un-churched. In the ten years that he has served there, church membership has grown by 300 percent. More importantly, it has grown in spiritual depth, because Conn sees his church as a spiritual gym—that is, as a space in which he coaches people to grow their spiritual lives. He challenges people to go deeper, stretch, and develop patterns of behavior that contribute to spiritual growth. He even compares these exercises to lifting weights: if you daily lift ten pounds with your right arm, your arm will get stronger. You don't have to believe that your arm will get stronger. It will. As he puts it, a similar thing happens with spiritual practices. If one exercises in this spiritual way, a person will grow stronger spiritually, even if they don't totally understand how or even believe that it's possible.

What would it look like if your congregation looked a bit more like a spiritual gym?

Mentors

In addition to highlighting the possibilities inherent in the role of a spiritual coach, there is also value in seeing clergy as mentors. We commend a book by Edward S. Little called *The Heart of the Leader*. This retired bishop speaks of leadership by reflecting on the relationship of Saint Paul and Timothy as recorded in the New Testament. That relationship may well have echoed Jesus's relationship with a relatively small group of disciples (there were only twelve, and in that group, there were a few distinctive relationships). There are limits to how many people a spiritual leader can mentor in this kind of close relationship. The role of mentor with a select few, however, is both possible and powerful. And that, in turn, allows for those people who have been in the mentoring relationship to mentor others.

How we think about the role of clergy matters. They are not monarchs. They are not CEOs. But, with a spirit of humility, they can serve as coaches or mentors, encouraging actual spiritual growth in their fields of service.

❖ How Are Clergy Sustained Spiritually?

This clarification of clergy roles leads us to ask how spiritual leaders may be supported and nourished in our communities. How many parish profiles have you read that led you to wonder if even Jesus would get a call back? How are we calling and supporting leaders? How can they be best equipped to do the work of forming disciples, focusing singularly on spiritual growth? Are we expecting too much from them? Are we expecting the wrong thing? Are demands on them excessive, unrealistic, or doomed to failure? If spiritual growth is the singular focus in congregational life, can our leaders be equipped and thereby freed to be a guide into spiritual growth?

While writing her book *Christianity after Religion,* Diana Butler Bass received this anonymous note from a member of the clergy, a note that points to a challenge all too common among those who have been at it for a while:

> After over twenty years of parish ministry, I am leaving it. I have resigned from all my denominational roles, and no one has said a word. Yet we are sad to leave, because of what it means. It means to us the church has become irrelevant to us. We care about spiritual disciplines of study, worship,

confession and forgiveness, discernment, fellowship, and mission. In the church, I spent more time discussing the replacement of the church roof than on discerning our purpose as a church. We miss the liturgy and the relationships, but I do not miss the constant bickering over meaningless garbage, evening meetings, and working every weekend.

This story is too common. It calls on the church to consider ways that clergy can be sustained in their ministries, staying in touch with their "first love"—that is, why they followed this vocational path. The whole community has a part to play in the edification of clergy, to build them up and not tear them down.

So what can be done to keep clergy nourished? For many clergy, one of the keys to spiritual growth is *finding colleague groups* that share more than just complaints about the bishop or disgruntled parishioners. Such sustaining communities could include the study of scripture, prayer, the sharing of life concerns, joys and challenges, losses and longings.

Clergy should also be able to make time and arrangements for their own *discipleship training,* including conferences, retreats, mentor relationships, and spiritual direction. Lay leaders should make sure that clergy, who often tend to work 24/7, take this time and avail themselves of such opportunities. This includes weekly time for sabbath, the gift of a time to recall one's identity (Abraham Heschel's book *The Sabbath* is most helpful here). For most clergy, Sunday is not that day of rest but rather their pivotal workday. So other times of the week must be set aside.

While the clergy leader certainly must make the effort to make their spiritual growth a priority, the vestry and other lay leaders also play a pivotal role. Their job is, in part, to support and encourage the clergy, providing resources to deepen their spiritual lives and establish patterns of care for them. In one church, the lay leaders, on a regular basis, asked the senior pastor this question: Is it well with your soul? One could imagine that question asked in an intrusive, judgmental, or evaluative way. But this pastor took it as genuine concern. It allowed her to think sincerely about the wellness of her soul, especially in those times when the well may be running dry.

At all times, the congregation is called to pray regularly for the clergy. In one church where the rector and vestry suffered a contentious relationship, members of the vestry even described themselves as "the loyal opposition," a euphemistic way of noting division. There must be another way. One of the best ways to deal with conflict and contention in communities is to pray for the person who causes us such angst.

For most congregations, this approach requires a shift in thinking. It can be a rare thing for a congregation or vestry to think about what it can do to nourish its leaders. We often assume such relationships only work the other way around—clergy nourishing the congregation. Recognizing that we all need spiritual growth, then, is a big step in the right direction.

We asked a couple of bishops about how they focus on keeping spiritually nourished. Prayer, exercise, and relationships emerged as significant themes in their responses. Bishop Thomas James Brown of the Diocese of Maine says the tradition of Morning Prayer sustains him. He finds it even more essential in his role as bishop.

Brown also describes his spiritual leadership like an engine. Sometimes its revolutions are too high, a source of concern is that he will overheat. Through physical exercise, then, he renews his energy while also quieting his spirit. Likewise, Bishop Rob Hirschfeld of the Diocese of New Hampshire spends time rowing and cycling—activities that take him away from cell phones, computers, or other media—for the sake of his body and soul. He adds that every significant epiphany, homily, and decision has come out of periods of such solitude, as he stares into space while moving through it.

Finally, relationships with others are critical to keeping spiritual leaders nourished. Hirschfeld has what he calls a "pit crew:" a spiritual director, a coach, a therapist, a curious and loving spouse, and a staff willing to challenge and correct him. Likewise, Brown relies on colleagues—diocesan staff, other bishops, and a clergy support group—for his spiritual nourishment. Brown is also quick to add that his marriage provides an immense source of nourishment, as his husband's tenderness, intellect, and faith are a remarkable mixture of balm and energy.

❖ What Kind of Leaders Does the Church Need?

To help answer these questions, consider a source from outside the church, a book written by Harry Kraemer, former president of Baxter Pharmaceutical. In his book *From Values to Action*, Kraemer articulates four values for leaders. While these principles are shaped by his engagement in a corporate setting, they may also apply to spiritual leadership.

According to Kraemer, effective leaders display the following characteristics:

1. *Self-reflection:* the ability to reflect and identify what one stands for, what one's values are and what matters most

2. *Balance and perspective:* the ability to see situations from multiple perspectives, including differing viewpoints to gain a holistic understanding

3. *True self-confidence:* the ability of a person to accept oneself as they are, recognizing strengths and weaknesses and focusing on continuing improvement

4. *Genuine humility:* the ability to appreciate the value of each person in the organization and to treat everyone respectfully.

While the church is not a business, these characteristics of successful secular leaders may offer some relevance for spiritual leaders. In our conversations with bishops, we asked them about the challenges facing spiritual leaders today, what they see working well among spiritual leaders in their diocese, the characteristics they are looking for in spiritual leaders today, and how congregations can identify individuals with those gifts.

Challenges facing spiritual leaders today

Bishop Mariann Edgar Budde of the Diocese of Washington points to the challenges that come with competing priorities, the energy required to sustain institutional demands, and overwhelming schedules. Spiritual leaders must, therefore, be able to set priorities and juggle a wide range of responsibilities.

Brown identifies two challenges: a perceived lack of need for God—akin to the complacency we discussed above—and the habit of looking in the rearview mirror. First, he says, leaders cannot easily foster spiritual growth in the face of communities that don't openly confess a need for redemption and renewal or where there is no expression of enthusiasm for the person, nature, and work of Jesus Christ. Secondly, all too often he hears statements like, "Bishop, we need to get back to the days when our Sunday School was bustling"—statements he attributes partly to nostalgia and partly to grief. While he understands and occasionally shares those feelings himself, he believes this retrospective inclination— even more commonplace in some communities due to the COVID-19 pandemic—holds us back from growing in the faith of Jesus Christ.

Hirschfeld notes three challenges. First, he identifies a significant shift in our religious culture whereby congregations are no longer the primary "delivery system" of Christianity in the United States. Most people derive their spiritual education and formation from blogs, podcasts, and social media feeds that transcend (or even challenge) traditional parochial boundaries. Thus, congregational leaders must either compete with spiritual superstars like Richard Rohr, Parker Palmer, Barbara Brown Taylor, Nadia Bolz-Weber, and Krista Tippett or integrate, engage, and converse in this widely permeable marketplace of religious and spiritual exchange.

Second is the challenge of remaining rooted, grounded, and stable in one's faith during a time of massive societal transformation. With change comes loss, and spiritual leaders must be able to navigate through such rocky shoals. Finally, many congregations still cling to the myth of "keeping everyone happy" by providing endlessly new programs and gimmicks to keep the show going. Hirschfeld notes that these are the same congregations where clergy stress has led to health crises or church discipline.

What's working well among spiritual leaders

Brown sees tremendous adaptation and energy among many spiritual leaders in the Diocese of Maine. Clergy, he reports, are feeding themselves and their congregations with a renewed hope for a church whose digital presence and witness is eclipsing pre-pandemic patterns. Zoom helps. Clergy gatherings once occurred in-person and required time, travel, and expense. But now his clergy gather as a diocesan community every fortnight, and they meet in regional groups online, leading to a greater sense of collegiality.

Hirschfeld also mentions collegiality as a key ingredient in current successes, adding that his heart was gladdened when a visiting bishop remarked upon the absence of competitiveness among the clergy of New Hampshire. Online meetings have helped in this regard, as throughout the COVID-19 pandemic he met with clergy to share updates, prayer requests, and topics of concern. He also mentions successes among bivocational congregations—that is, churches with part-time clergy who also have other secular jobs. In part out of necessity, these churches have equipped the ministry of all the baptized, therefore allowing priests the ability to focus on being priests rather than "cruise ship activities directors."

Necessary characteristics in spiritual leaders today

Budde insists that spiritual leaders must have a compelling faith; a vision for a vital, robust church; a willingness to face the hard truths of our systemic decline; the capacity for strategic action; perseverance; emotional maturity; and self-regulation. She stresses the importance of having multicultural and racially diverse clergy. Her diocese has produced a diocesan profile that names this as a priority. (See the appendix for what the diocese is looking for in clergy and what the diocese believes contributes to congregational vitality.) Budde also believes that clergy should be mission-focused, entrepreneurial, collaborative, and adaptive.

When looking for clergy for the Diocese of Maine, Brown seeks, first, those with a joyous love for Jesus Christ, and he is quick to admit that this can take any number of forms. Brown says such joy is more than mere happiness or jollity (which often depends on favorable but fleeting circumstances) but rather a "vibrant resilience" deriving from faith that Jesus's resurrection truly triumphs over evil, death, and hopelessness. On this basis, Brown carefully discerns whether candidates have a warm heart for ministry, a spirit that invites others to engage in ministry, and the ways in which they incarnate the goodness of the Lord in their lives.

Second, like Budde's insistence on emotional maturity and self-regulation, Brown looks for those with deep self-knowledge of their strengths, weaknesses, privileges, and vulnerabilities. This includes the capacity to be at home in silence, not overly dependent upon positive feedback, and having sufficient inner strength to withstand being outside the center of attention.

Echoing Budde's observations regarding entrepreneurial and adaptive characteristics, Brown adds that he looks and listens for leaders who are innovative. The ability to adapt to changing circumstances and a love for learning new things are key.

Finally, he is eager to welcome clergy who love the region, its geography and culture, and those who can name potential opportunities there sooner than they can describe the pitfalls. (We'll read more about this in Chapter 6, "Pastor the Community.")

The ABCs of Spiritual Leadership

Affection. Brevity. Curiosity. Diligence. Elan. Fortitude.
Gravitas. Humility. Industry. Joy. Knowledge.
Level-headedness. Motivation. Nobility. Optimism. Piety.
Quietness. Resilience. Stamina. Tech-embracing. Understanding.
Vulnerable. Warmth. X-centric. Yielding. Zest.

—Bishop Thomas James Brown

✤ ✤ ✤

❖ How Can the Vestry and Other Lay Leaders Promote Spiritual Growth?

In most congregations, if you were to ask who the spiritual leader is, the answer would be the rector. That's fitting. The clergy leader (rector or priest-in-charge) might well be regarded as CSO (chief spiritual officer). But that person is not the only one who bears the privilege and responsibility of spiritual leadership. The healthiest congregational systems share the mantle of spiritual leadership with various lay leaders—wardens, vestry members, and others—all of whom are called to champion with single-mindedness the spiritual growth of the parish.

If you want to trigger a deer-in-the-headlights look from a member of the vestry, speak to them about being a spiritual leader. In many places, vestry members are selected because they know how to read a financial statement, have experience dealing with contractors, or have access to significant donors. Some are selected because they are popular in the congregation or the community. But how is a faith community changed when the lay leaders are seen as spiritual leaders?

It is vital for clergy and parishioners to recognize that clergy are not the only spiritual leaders in a congregation. The vestry should be seen as modeling spiritual growth and development as well, and those serving in this capacity must include spiritual nourishment as part of the experience. While individual vestry members bring specific expertise to the group (with backgrounds in finance, management, building administration, communications, and so on), the rector should focus on using the vestry experience to further everyone's spiritual journey— much in the way that Jesus focused on forming his disciples. This focus will create and empower lay leadership. For this to happen, clergy—and lay leaders—must embrace the vision that they are all spiritual leaders. Sometimes clergy must be convinced that this is a good idea. And sometimes that's an uphill climb.

Bishop Eugene Sutton of the Diocese of Maryland insists that the future of the Episcopal Church lies with the lay leadership, adding that clergy lose authority when they exert excessive control: "We have religious institutions, some whole denominations, and certainly parishes that are invested in keeping their people at a low level of spiritual development and human and intellectual development. The leader exercises the power.... [but] you've got to let the people grow up. You talk about lay leadership and why we don't have lay leadership? One reason is that [they're being kept] in a system of control and not [being allowed to] rise up!"

If Sutton's analysis is right, how might the clergy help lay leaders to rise up? One example of a pathway forward was developed by Dawn Davis, an experienced Anglican priest in Canada who directs the Leadership for Ministry program at Huron University. With a background in human resources and specializations in training, development, and organizational behavior, Davis developed a program called *Revive* while she was serving as a rector. It was her way to help parishes facilitate growth in spiritual vitality. A listing of that program's stated goals helps identify how we may lift up lay leaders to encourage spiritual growth in our communities. During the *Revive* program, participants:

- develop a prayer life that suits their personal spiritual temperament;
- gain confidence in speaking about God in their lives;
- experience scripture as a spiritual resource;
- gain experience praying in public and leading Bible study;
- create a Rule of Life that expresses their personal spiritual practices; and
- discern their call for justice, forgiveness, and peace as servants of Christ's kingdom.

Clergy who have led this program in their parishes report seeing even their own spiritual lives flourish as they reignite their "first love" and calling. To offer lay leaders a deeper relationship with the living, grace-filled, loving God is perhaps the most important and transformative gift any spiritual leader can offer long-serving and dedicated servants of the church.

What Are Some Practical Ways to Lead for Spiritual Growth?

As congregations move to greater focus on spiritual growth, there are some simple things leaders can do to make a cultural shift in that direction. These need not involve new programs, expanded staffing, or additional line items in the operating budget. In many ways, simple steps can make subtle shifts in work that is already ongoing. Here we suggest ten such steps, but perhaps you may think of others:

1. *Surround the meeting with prayer.* It's a simple thing to do. Simply decide that every gathering will begin and end with prayer. It can be a prayer from the Book of Common Prayer or some other resource. Or participants can be encouraged, maybe even challenged, to offer a prayer of their own crafting. In all these gatherings, however, avoid having the clergy be the sole professional pray-er.

2. *Embed scripture in every gathering.* The reader will find this to be a consistent theme in this book. Incorporating scripture into every gathering drives home the important point that we are people guided by a common text. We believe the Spirit speaks through the text, even passages that are baffling or unsettling. Again, this can be as simple as reading one verse, or even just a single phrase, and briefly reflecting on it. Or it can be a more extensive study. Embedding scripture in everything is one of the five best practice principles so we'll visit this again in Chapter 4.

3. *Frame all the work the church does as ministry.* Perhaps using the Outline of the Faith, consider the role described for the ministers of the church starting on page 855 of the Book of Common Prayer. The ministers of the church are all the people. Everything we do in church is considered ministry or service. This approach frames the work of the church in a new way, not as a task to be done, but as an offering. It's not the work of the professionals; it's everyone's work. (See Brian McLaren's piece entitled Everyone is Clergy, found in Chapter 5 and in the appendix.) Scripture and prayer are critical parts of this framing. Regular commissioning of lay ministers in the context of worship helps to underscore this theme of service.

4. *Equip the saints for ministry.* The leader plays an important role in establishing and supporting this new culture of seeing all the work of the church as ministry. In Paul's Letter to the Ephesians, he writes about equipping the saints for ministry: "The gifts [God] gave were that some would be apostles, some prophets, some evangelists, some pastors and teachers, to equip the saints for the work of ministry, for building up the body of Christ, until all of us come to the unity of the faith and of the knowledge of the Son of God, to maturity, to the measure of the full stature of Christ" (Ephesians 4:11-13). How does this play out in our congregations today? What do people need in that regard? How can the leader-as-coach challenge and

encourage all the saints? What training and feedback can be offered? What expectations are clearly articulated?

5. ***Develop leaders.*** Many, if not most, people attribute their engagement with the church as the direct result of a personal invitation. This is a much more effective tool than an announcement in a bulletin. The leader should always be looking for new leaders. The mentor role can be key in this development. The leader should be on the lookout for encouraging and developing new leaders. Further, in a denomination that still remains segregated along lines of race and class, the leader should look for diversity represented in leadership. In that regard, developing leaders also becomes a matter of social justice, a growth edge for most mainline congregations.

6. ***Deepen relationships among leaders.*** The church is ultimately about relationships, a reflection of our commitment to the doctrine of the Trinity, which says that God is by nature a relationship. Leaders are called to steward relationships within the congregation and to keep lines of communication open. They are to practice appreciative inquiry and celebrate diversity. In meetings, they allow for time in meetings for everyone to speak, making a commitment to avoid triangulation or parking lot meetings. One simple way to do this with vestry members is to assign prayer partners, so that each year, vestry members commit to pray for each other.

7. ***Practice accountability and elevate expectations.*** As vestry members come to understand their role as spiritual leaders, it will be important to find ways to hold each other accountable. This may mean developing vestry covenants or other tools to hold members of the group accountable.

8. ***Anticipate resistance and conflict.*** One adage says that Jesus came to comfort the afflicted and afflict the comfortable. A singular focus on spiritual growth is bound to present

challenges to those who have grown comfortable with their congregation, even if it is not a sustainable model. Spiritual leaders will anticipate the challenge and not shy away from it.

9. *Honor people's presence and participation.* This is simple—but often ignored. Say thank you to people for their offerings. Better yet, say, "Thanks be to God." Make sure to recognize their contributions, commission them in some form, and allow them to complete their tasks. Many fear taking on a leadership role because they regard it as a life sentence. Let people fulfill their tasks for a season and then find creative ways to say: "Well done, thou good and faithful servant."

10. *Practice joy.* The American journalist H. L. Mencken described a puritan as someone who is unhappy because somebody somewhere is having a good time. Too often that is the message communicated by religious people. What can you do to foster a spirit of joy in the life of your congregation, in your worship experience, even in church meetings? G. K. Chesterton, an English author and theologian, said that angels can fly because they take themselves lightly. The work of the church can be difficult, no doubt. But spiritually vital congregations find a way to live into the injunction from Saint Paul in his letter to the Philippians: "Rejoice in the Lord always."

Let us return to the witness of scripture to sum up our reflections on the heart of the leader, acknowledging the distinctive way that the biblical tradition regards qualification for leadership. Moses's call came in the wilderness where he was tending sheep, a far cry from Pharaoh's splendid home where Moses would have received excellent training in leadership. When Moses hears the voice calling to him from the burning bush, he turns aside to check it out and responds: "Here am I." As he grasps the scope of the call to confront Pharaoh, however, Moses soon responds: *Who am I? Who am I to take on this task? You've got the wrong guy!* In the face of challenges, he doesn't see himself as qualified. The response from the Holy One does not list Moses's attributes but simply says: "I will be with you."

Similarly, when Jeremiah hears a call in the first chapter of the book attributed to him, he declines, saying he's just a youngster. The holy response: "I will be with you." Peter, who never has an unexpressed thought, is not a particularly gifted fisherman (it appears he never caught a fish without Jesus's help). He asks Jesus to leave him alone because he sees himself as a sinful man, one who vacillates between bold affirmation of faith and shameful denial. How can this be the rock on which Jesus builds his community?

And consider Paul's words describing leadership in his first letter to the Corinthians: "Let no one boast about human leaders, for all things are yours, whether Paul or Apollos or Cephas or the world or life or death or the present or the future—all belong to you, and you belong to Christ, and Christ belongs to God" (1 Corinthians 3:21-23).

These witnesses and many others underscore the important theme of the heart of the leader, the need for the leader to develop an ongoing relationship of trust in God's graceful presence, claiming God's power to do great things in us and through us and even in spite of us.

Questions
for Reflection

One of the great challenges for Episcopal congregations is to arrive at consensus that the mission of the congregation has to do with making disciples. Is that the mission of your congregation? Should it be? What are the challenges and opportunities in embracing that kind of focus?

If you are a leader in a congregation, how are you being supported? Where do you find nourishment? What are ways to avoid burnout?

How can leaders stay in touch with their "first love," the thing that got them into ministry in the first place?

How can congregants support their leaders?

The Heart of the Leader

3

Get People Moving

If one of the roles of a congregational leader is to serve as spiritual coach, what is the goal of all that coaching? We find an answer in the next best practice principle, which is to *get people moving*. It presumes that movement is part of the spiritual journey—and, indeed, that such movement is a desired objective.

We base this principle on the conviction that the spiritual health of our denomination is a function of the spiritual health of the dioceses in that denomination, which is, in turn, a function of the spiritual health of congregations in that diocese, which is, yet again, a function of the spiritual health of the individuals in those congregations. We call it the cellular model of spiritual vitality. It's a model offered in the awareness that many church institutions (denominational structures, diocesan entities, congregations) are inert, resistant to change, unmovable. The cellular model, however, holds that vitality can spring from grassroots. It is important, then, to ask: Are the individuals in our congregations, especially including its leaders, growing spiritually? Are they aware of being on a spiritual journey? If the answer is yes, then this focus on spiritual growth will make a difference in the vitality of the congregation. If not, how do we get moving on that journey?

Through our research and consultations with several hundred Episcopal churches, we have discovered that one cannot assume that people are interested in movement, in spiritual growth. Many people have no idea that this kind of growth is possible for them, let alone desirable. Far too many in our pews give a blank stare when asked about a spiritual journey. So, as a starting point in our discussion of "getting people moving," it's important to understand why such movement matters.

Brian McLaren, a gifted pastor, teacher, and astute observer of the current state of the church in America, says the life-and-death question for each of our churches and denominations may boil down to this: Are we a club for the elite who pretend to have arrived or a school for disciples who are still on the way? In other words, is movement key to what the church is and does? Perhaps another way to get at this point is to ask whether the spiritual life is a destination or a journey.

Many of our churches function as clubs, restrictive in nature, even if that is not explicitly stated. There is nothing inherently wrong with the idea of a club or with the social nature of the church, though that "clubbiness" has been a pretext for exclusion. But the church must be more than a social gathering. It must be a community of transformation. This notion can be a culture change for many congregations, presenting them with a challenge to think differently about their purpose. Consider the comment of one parishioner who couldn't fathom such talk of movement: "I don't know why you all are talking about spiritual growth. I don't expect anything to happen to me when I come to church."

Church-growth scholar Zscheile poses the question in another way, in the introduction to his book *People of the Way*. He asks: "What does it mean to be a member? What does it mean to be a disciple? Are they the same thing?" One rector told the story of receiving an invitation to a dinner party from a person who was not a member of her congregation. After more than five years serving as leader of this congregation, she was excited about the opportunity to gather with others who might not even know she was local clergy. She could enjoy an evening without hearing complaints about the liturgy or the bulletins or the landscaping at the church. Just a night out. As she arrived at the home, she met an interesting fellow with an exciting international career. They began to talk, moved through the buffet line, sat together, continuing the conversation about this gentleman's interesting work. At some point, the conversation turned and the guy who had been doing all the talking asked the rector: "And what do you do?" Upon responding that she was the rector of the local Episcopal church, she was stunned to hear the man exclaim: "Well, that's my church!" The rector had been there for five years and yet had never met this parishioner. What was perhaps more shocking, however, was that this engaging dinner partner did not find this revelation such a shock. Sure, that church was where he and his family took part in baptisms, confirmation, weddings, and where his funeral would eventually take place, but ongoing discipleship wasn't on his radar.

❖ What Do Scripture and Tradition Say About Getting People Moving?

As we consider this best practice principle, it's helpful to explore the ways that scripture speaks about movement in the spiritual life. In the book of Genesis, for instance, Adam and Eve leave the garden and launch the biblical narrative of God in relationship with God's people and creation. Soon, we meet Abraham and Sarah who set out from their comfortable home to find a new God-given place (Genesis 12–25). Abraham and Sarah move, not knowing where they are going (Hebrews 11:8-12), which is the way life unfolds for a lot of us. In Exodus, Moses leads the children of Israel from Egypt to the promised land, a journey marked by both challenge and formation. Later in the Old Testament, the experience of exile focuses on how to find a way home.

Moving to the narrative of the New Testament, Jesus leads a group of disciples from town to town, teaching as he goes, never settling down. He describes himself as the way, and so the first Christians called themselves "people of the way." And his parting word to them in the Gospel of Matthew is "Go!" They receive God's grace, for sure, but that does not mean they have arrived. In the Letter to the Ephesians, we read: "For by grace you have been saved through faith, and this is not your own doing; it is the gift of God—not the result of works, so that no one may boast. For we are what he has made us, created in Christ Jesus for good works, which God prepared beforehand to be our way of life" (Ephesians 2:8-10).

Grace is a given, but that grace is by no means a destination. Grace is essential, because without it, growth will not happen. But that grace is meant to launch a new way of life, a journey of walking into the good works God has prepared. As writer Anne Lamott admits, "I do not understand the mystery of grace—only that it meets us where we are and does not leave us where it found us." Such movement implies action, and thus we read in the Letter of James that faith without works is dead. We are not only to experience the movement of transformation in our own lives, but also our grace-based faith is intended to change the world. The Diocese of Ohio put it this way in a billboard to proclaim their faith: "Love God. Love Neighbor. Change the World."

This theme of movement is reflected in our liturgy as well. The service of Holy Eucharist begins with procession. We stand and sit and kneel—Episcopal aerobics that can require adeptness at book juggling! We march the gospel, our central story, into the center of the people, to signal its importance. The priest celebrates with manual acts, with movement of the body. We come forward to receive the bread and wine, perhaps an Anglican version of an altar call. We retire in procession, with the words of the dismissal commissioning us to go out into the world to love and serve the Lord with gladness and singleness of heart. That commissioning may well be the most important part of the liturgy.

In addition, the promises made in baptism found in the Book of Common Prayer, starting on page 304, begin with a call to life in the community ("Will you continue in the apostle's teaching...?"). But that is just the starting point. This life in a community, marked as it is by grace and forgiveness, is intended for movement beyond the walls of the church. We are to proclaim good news in word and action. We are to seek and serve Christ in all persons, not just all congregants, not just all Episcopalians. We are to strive for justice and peace and respect the dignity of every human being. To fulfill these promises, we must be on the move. The verbs in the prayers for the baptismal candidate include a call to movement, as we pray for the candidate sent into the world in witness to God's love (The Book of Common Prayer, p. 305).

As this book was written, we were in the throes of the COVID-19 pandemic, which brought coincident crises of health, economics, and racial division. These crises brought to light inequities in our society, making more urgent than ever the need to get people moving, to motivate the people of God to strive for justice and peace. This is a call for the whole church. As Pope Francis said in a homily: "There's no such thing as a stationary Christian.... A stationary Christian is sick in his or her identity." Perhaps this expectation of movement and growth is why the verb "Go" is included in the Way of Love initiative defined by Presiding Bishop Curry. Scripture and tradition tell us that there is nothing static about our faith.

❖ How Do We Get People Moving?

What does movement look like in a congregation? Let's begin with the basics: welcoming newcomers to our communities of faith, communities that by definition are places where people are called to grow, laboratories for spiritual development, gyms for spiritual exercises. The dirty little secret is that many churches aren't really all that interested in growth or transformation—unless, of course, that leads to more pledging units or more people to serve on committees. One woman engaged in a conversation about spiritual growth and welcoming new members said: "I don't know why you all are talking about welcoming new people. Everyone who ought to be an Episcopalian in town already is." When congregations experience growth in membership (which doesn't happen as often as it should), we occasionally hear that long-tenured parishioners are rattled with the arrival of newcomers. The longtime members want to know everyone's name. They fear that these new people will change things. Coffee hour, if any newcomers dare join, can be a brutally lonely experience, as friends cluster and newcomers look for the exit. Almost every parish profile notes that their church is a welcoming place, but those profiles are invariably created by those who are on the inside.

When there is already an expectation of movement or growth or transformation, however, the congregation has a culture of readiness for welcome, an expectation of the new thing God wants to do in the community. But when that expectation is absent, a church can become like a stagnant pond with no new life flowing in. And ponds like that sometimes begin to stink. Things growing in those ponds sometimes die. The fact is that our churches are not always as welcoming as we imagine or hope. That is especially true when we recognize that 11 a.m. on Sunday morning is still the most segregated hour in the week. Welcoming all is not only an issue of hospitality—it's an issue of justice.

I drew a cartoon that tells the story of a newcomer couple who made the mistake of sitting in the pew of an established parishioner at the 8 a.m. service. The longtime member greets the couple warmly, "Welcome. So glad you're here," then she says, "Oh, by the way, you're in my pew." When the cartoon was posted on social media, someone immediately commented, criticizing the drawing and claiming it was an unfair caricature of the Episcopal Church. The critic added, "This would never happen." With that, people from around the globe responded that it had, in fact, happened to them. Especially poignant was the person who remembered it happening to her twenty years ago; she never returned to that church. We will not get people moving in the journey of faith if we put up obstacles for the people who seek to take first steps into the community.

Toward the end of his letter to the Romans, Saint Paul writes: "Welcome one another....just as Christ has welcomed you" (Romans 15:7). To get people moving in the spiritual journey, we must focus on the quality of welcome. Is it done in the spirit of Jesus? What is the experience of welcome in your community? An evaluation can be done in very simple terms: looking at signage, reviewing the bulletins to see how user-friendly they are, and creating a culture in which everyone is a greeter rather than appointing a specific team. Other measures include evaluating the church's presence online. Given that most people now find a new church home on the internet, it's worth asking what your church's website says about welcome. St. James' Church on Madison Avenue in New York provides a great example of how to get people moving on their first online visit. Instead of a static presentation touting programs and activities, the homepage is an invitation to a spiritual journey, making a point that is repeated throughout the community: everyone is on a spiritual journey, a journey that matters to God, a journey that therefore matters to the community.

At this church, a message of welcome is underscored by the announcements made each week by the rector as the service begins. The rector welcomes everyone to the gathering, adding that if anyone is interested in talking about their own spiritual journey, she will meet them right after the service at a designated (and obvious) location for that conversation. She invites everyone to fill out an information card that has the title: Start here! From the first encounter with this congregation, there is a possibility, indeed an expectation, of growth.

A wonderful program currently taking hold in the Episcopal Church is Invite Welcome Connect. This is a ministry of "relational evangelism and congregational empowerment allowing churches to become places of genuine connection for inviting the faith journeys and stories of everyone, enabling deeper journeys of Christian discipleship and enabling the Spirit of Christ to be at the heart of each church's hospitable mission of spreading the good news." That's a mouthful, but its point is that spiritual growth requires concrete action. Matt Holcombe, rector of St. Michael's Church in Colorado Springs, says Invite Welcome Connect gets people moving "by changing the ethos of a church from 'maintenance mode' to empowering congregations to utilize the gifts idling sitting in the pews."

It's notable that the title of the initiative contains three verbs, words that denote something to do: invite, welcome, and connect. The initiative's website clarifies each of these verbs in turn: inviting involves evangelism, welcome implies hospitality, and connections create belonging. But "evangelism, hospitality, and belonging" all too often become buzzwords that fail to buzz. The verbs "invite, welcome, and connect" communicate what we must actually do to move out of maintenance mode. In order to start people moving, one of the things we must do with our language is to focus our talk around actions rather than states of being so that newcomers know what to expect.

It's a beautiful thing for churches to say, "Come as you are." The unconditional aspect of that welcome reflects the message of grace at the heart of our faith. Our world hungers for that kind of welcome. At the same time, many people who seek to engage with a community are eager to know what is expected of them. Indeed, they want to be challenged. People go to yoga sessions, gyms, and classes of all kinds to be changed, to be challenged, and to grow in some way. Churches must offer that kind of experience, too. Otherwise, why should anyone bother? Consider a few examples, then, of how some Episcopal churches have guided people into deeper engagement not only with the community but also in their relationship with God in Christ.

Newcomer gatherings

One way to challenge newcomers in helpful ways is to establish an expectation that all parishioners—newcomers and old-timers and everyone in between—take part in a member incorporation class, sometimes called an inquirers' or newcomers' class. This class can be offered seasonally, tailored to a one-time presentation, or turned into an ongoing small group that runs all year long. A critical element of this gathering, however, is to invite people to share their own story, their spiritual biographies. In addition, there should be engaging teaching and discussions on the roles of scripture, tradition, reason and experience. Understanding the role of baptism and the eucharist in spiritual growth is important, and introduction to the Book of Common Prayer as a resource for spiritual practice is key. This teaching is a great opportunity for newcomers. But the truth is that many people have been attending church for years and have not learned this material. The work of evangelism in Episcopal churches often begins with people who are already on our membership rolls. Such gatherings, then, should aim to provide a context where people can experience community and to offer easily identifiable marks that help them understand what the community is about. These gatherings may also serve as an opportunity to draw in those who at one time were part of the parish community but have drifted into wide orbit. Statistics indicate there are a lot of those floating around the Episcopal Church.

Parish partners

Hillary Raining, rector of St. Christopher's Church in Gladwynne, Pennsylvania, describes one of the ways in which her church welcomes newcomers: "We have a membership committee that helps congregants find their vocation. When someone new joins the parish, they are assigned a parish partner to help them get active in the parish in the first year. Additionally, we continually help people who have been members for years become more engaged in ministries they may not have considered yet." The work of the committee provides a great example of mentoring, which we spoke about in the previous chapter on the heart of the leader, but it transfers the role of mentor from clergy to lay people. It also celebrates the dignity of each newcomer, recognizing that each person comes with gifts. How will those gifts be put to use? How will a newcomer feel about the community when their gifts are recognized and applied to the life of the church?

Starting with service

Another church was promoting a food drive for their pantry, so they came up with a slogan to reflect the idea that every parishioner could participate, no matter their age or income level or level of engagement with the church. They made the bet that everybody could bring a can of food to church. People liked the idea, so they made it a slogan to cover all aspects of mission and outreach, with the expectation that being part of the community meant being of service. Guided by their slogan, "Everyone can" the church made opportunities available, clearly communicating ways for newcomers (and everyone!) to get involved in service. While newcomers to the Episcopal Church may have questions and doubts about church doctrines, most people bring no objection to the idea of service, which is one of the ways we follow Jesus. Varied opportunities for service provide an excellent on-ramp for people to journey further in the life of the community and in their own love of God and neighbor.

❖ How Do We Get People Moving *Again*?

Getting people moving certainly has a lot to do with welcoming new people to the church. But there are those who have been in the pews for decades who need to get moving as well. How do we get those members launched along the spiritual journey (again)? It's a matter of getting them to recognize spiritual growth as a value, providing similar on-ramps for journeying with the community, and nurturing a deeper sense of God's presence in their lives. That value has not always been preached or taught.

As we've seen, this principle of spiritual movement has to do with inviting, welcoming, and connecting, but it's also about so much more. It suggests incorporation, in the literal sense of how members are more deeply incorporated into the body of Christ. While this is important for newcomers, it is also important for those who have been in the Episcopal Church for decades, many of whom have shifted into disengagement and infrequent attendance. This focus on incorporation is important too for those known as the Christmas and Easter crowd, those who are in wide orbit, affectionately referred to as *plutos*. For these folks (and every congregation has them), the community has some gravitational pull, so there is an opportunity to drawn them closer to the center. Often though, something stands in the way. Leaders face the challenge of figuring out how to tap into that holy gravitational energy and how to remove obstacles that have perpetuated such distance.

Our research indicates that Episcopalians are long-tenured. Many have been in the church for years. Yet, as we shared, more than 60 percent remain in the first stages of spiritual growth. Many have never wrapped their minds around the idea that they are on a spiritual journey. In one congregation where the Spiritual Life Inventory was offered, a parishioner confessed that he had been in the congregation for more than forty years and had seen rectors come and go, each with some kind of congregational survey every five years. He said the surveys asked all kinds of things, like when service times would be most convenient or what they should do to improve the kitchen or what kind of parking lot would be most helpful (direct or diagonal spaces). But the Spiritual Life Inventory was the first time anyone had inquired about his prayer life or whether some parts of the Bible meant more to him than others. Indeed, it is easy to hang around a church a long time without reflecting upon our journey, without considering whether we are stalled, have a flat tire, or have simply gotten lost along the way.

Wherever people find themselves in the spiritual journey, they tend to want to know about next steps. Leaders are called to make sure there are ways for newcomers and long-tenured congregants to grow in faith. These opportunities for spiritual growth come in the shape of teaching, preaching, and other types of communication. Presiding Bishop Curry has set an excellent example of this in promoting the Way of Love, an initiative with seven verbs forming a Rule of Life, or a way to live and practice our faith. Scott Gunn, an Episcopal priest and executive director of Forward Movement, has written an outstanding book, *The Way of Love: A Practical Guide,* offering accessible and tangible ways to incorporate these verbs into your daily life. Another excellent program has been produced by the Presiding Bishop's Office. It's called *My Way of Love.* It offers eight weeks of a spiritual plan, following an online inventory that explores the individual's beliefs, practices, and ways that individual puts faith into action. There are many similar programs, all indicating that people are hungry for guidance.

As leaders provide such on-ramps, however they often must clear the path, getting rid of obstacles to spiritual growth. One priest serving in a large city told a story of leading a weekday noon eucharist. Businesspeople, some who knew little about the Episcopal Church and some who knew little about the church at all, attended, drawn to the beauty of the sacred space and the quiet. As the priest led the service, he guided people with page numbers for the Book of Common Prayer. One regular attender, who had the service memorized, finally chastised him, saying that he didn't need to mention page numbers. As deeply religious as this person of faith was, however, he did not see the ways in which this priest was seeking to clear the pathway for people who might not be in the same place along their spiritual journey.

The power of small groups

A key to getting people moving in their own spiritual lives is to recognize that the spiritual life is more than what happens for an hour on Sunday. One of the best ways to make that connection is to encourage people to complement attendance at worship, which is at the heart of all we do, with some other growth opportunity when they are not at church. This can include personal spiritual practices, to be sure, but it often includes connection with a small group where issues of faith can be discussed with openness and trust.

The Episcopal Church has much to learn from megachurches. Episcopalians often roll their eyes at the thought of worshipping in a church with thousands of people. Many Episcopalians in small congregations imagine they would be lost or overlooked in such places. But many of these large communities attest to the fact that the key to their vitality is the incorporation of small groups. Many large churches even require their members to participate in a small group. These small groups provide a powerful complement to worship. Truth be told, as beautiful as the Episcopal liturgy is, it offers little opportunity for discussion, let alone heartfelt conversation or the sharing of life experience. You could come to worship for decades without anyone knowing your name or your story. Small groups, whatever form they take, can provide the opportunity for interaction, engagement, and support.

There are multiple ways to structure these groups. Many churches adapt a system that works for their context. One church had an extremely vital men's group with more than thirty people in regular attendance. They met at 6:15 a.m. because it fit the commuter schedule. Another church had a small group called Old Dogs—again, a men's group, but one intended for those seventy years and older. Christ Church in Charlotte, North Carolina, has developed its own program, "Christian Essentials," which highlights basics of the faith. While it was shaped for that particular congregation, they are glad to share the curriculum with others who might want to use this tool.

In recent years, programs like the Alpha Course have proven effective in connecting people with the congregation, with a community. Alpha's method includes gathering for a meal, a brief presentation on one of ten basic questions about the faith, and then table discussion about these questions. Frankly, the program does not work without the meal and the discussions. Forward Movement has created a similar small-group program called *Transforming Questions*, which is often used as preparation for baptism and confirmation in addition to basic adult formation. *Transforming Questions* is a ten-session course designed to help both new Christians and longtime churchgoers move into a deeper life in Christ.

Congregations as learning communities

Much of what this book discusses can be referred to as discipleship, but that word can be off-putting or mystifying. People may not know what we mean by the term. Sure, those fishermen were the first disciples. But what does it mean to be a disciple today? Arriving at a sufficient definition is one of the great creative tasks for leaders, but an important component of that definition is the idea of disciple as a student, a learner. No matter where we are in the spiritual journey, we are never done learning. God always has more to share with us.

Our research shows that Episcopalians seem particularly interested in learning about some specific topics. These embedded interests offer fruitful opportunities for clergy to fulfill their vocation as teachers as set forth in the service of ordination.

Ryan Fleenor, who served at St. James, Madison Avenue before accepting a call as rector of St. Luke's in Darien, Connecticut, developed a program to explore prayer. For forty days, a biblical precedent, he taught about prayer. He writes: "The whole idea of forty days was to invite people into the life of prayer but set ourselves up to say this is what we are doing from now on. So, if it turned out that people were interested in daily morning prayer or centering prayer, those things could continue. If they faded over the course of this time, we could discontinue them without anyone feeling like they or we had failed. It also meant people could try things on without feeling they had made an endless commitment."

The Book of Common Prayer is important connective tissue for the Episcopal Church and Anglican tradition, and it provides rich reflection for every season of life. It is a wonderfully rich resource for teaching about prayer.

The liturgy of Holy Eucharist is described in our prayer book as our principal act of worship, and our research with Episcopal churches shows that it is indeed a key catalyst for spiritual growth. While the eucharist is filled with mystery, there is still so much that we can do to grow in understanding of this central sacrament. For instance, leaders might incorporate instructed eucharists—that is, eucharists that include some teaching moments throughout—regularly in the Sunday schedule (ideally quarterly).

❖ What Are Some Other Practical Ways to Get People Moving?

The spiritual rearview mirror

Another powerful way to get people moving is to help them recognize that God has already been at work in their lives—and that transformation may have already taken place. We often say that the way to understand the spiritual journey and the good news of God's activity in each of our lives is to look in the spiritual rearview mirror. This can be done in an exercise that asks people to review their lives on a timeline, noting those times when God seemed close and when God seemed far away.

This activity can be done in small groups, where people write their own spiritual autobiographies and share them or they simply tell their stories. Clergy have often crafted these autobiographies numerous times for themselves, as it's often a standard part of the path to ordination and a part of other programs such as the popular Education for Ministry. But for many parishioners, creation of a spiritual autobiography is a novel idea. Offering the opportunity for congregants to craft their own spiritual autobiography can bear great fruit. People love to tell their stories.

It's important to note that these exercises to get people moving and engaged in spiritual growth can come with some challenges. Our churches are filled with people who have been wounded by religious institutions and experiences. The Episcopal Church, with its call to inclusion, has been a refuge for many people from other Christian traditions that have not been welcoming to people for any number of reasons (race, ethnicity, sexual orientation, and so on). But the Episcopal Church has also disappointed people. When people say that the church is full of hypocrites, all we can say is "guilty as charged." When we hear people say they don't like organized religion, we're inclined to joke: "Come to the Episcopal Church. We're not all that organized!" But the wounds are real and deep. They often stand in the way of spiritual growth. In this regard, getting people moving may need to begin with a healing process.

God sightings

Another tool to get people moving is to ask them to name how God is active in the present. Where do people see God at work in their own lives, occupations, churches, and communities, day in and day out?

Offer opportunities for people to share what they've seen and invite them to keep their eyes open for God's activity. This may be a cultural shift for your congregation, but it brings to the fore an elevated expectation that God does actually work in our lives. This kind of perspective can transform a ministry. Recall the church thrift store described in Chapter 1, in which many volunteers were on the verge of burnout. The ministry was transformed when the group decided to take time between the morning and afternoon shifts, when volunteers overlapped, to share with one another where they had seen God that morning and what they hoped to see in the afternoon.

A common text

Another way to get people moving is by having everyone in the parish read a book together. *Being Christian* by Rowan Williams; *Life Together* by Dietrich Bonhoeffer; *Jesus and the Disinherited*, by Howard Thurman, and *The Church Cracked Open* by Stephanie Spellers are all examples of books that have proven helpful for church reading groups. Of course countless others can be chosen based on your church's spiritual goals. Offer opportunities both in-person and online to discuss such books, share learnings, and discuss how the texts intersect with people's lives.

Give a gift!

Instead of a coffee mug or a t-shirt, give a copy of Chris Yaw's *Jesus Was an Episcopalian (And You Can Be One Too!)* to every new member. This book offers an engaging, lighthearted introduction to the Episcopal Church, focusing on the roles of scripture, tradition, and reason. It successfully demonstrates how our ancient faith has relevance for contemporary culture. There are, of course, other introductions to the Episcopal Church, so if that book does not seem to fit your community, find another resource to give new members.

Ministry invitation

Invite every ministry in the church to be explicit in identifying spiritual on-ramps for newcomers to launch their journeys in the life of the community. For those whose spiritual journeys have stalled or who have disengaged, these on-ramps can provide a critical way back into the life of a vital community. One church, for instance, always keeps an empty chair present at its meetings, an indication that they are always expecting new members to be part of the conversation. Communication tools like a website or weekly emails from clergy can help make sure these points of entry are always identifiable and accessible. But remember: nothing is as effective as a personal invitation.

Daily devotional

Provide ways for people to begin to read scripture on their own. Encourage a daily quiet time, same time, same chair, same duration, and a good cup of coffee. Give copies of a daily devotional like *Forward Day by Day* or *Daily Bread* to every parishioner and challenge them to use it daily. Encourage journaling, including writing down questions that can be taken to the clergy or other spiritual leaders in the church. In one church, the altar guild discussed how their ministry could grow in the coming year, so they decided to challenge their members to read *Forward Day by Day* each day. It forged a bond in the group that had not been there before, as they then shared how certain devotions affected their daily lives.

Annual retreat

When we speak with folks about when they experienced spiritual growth in their lives, many cite a retreat of some sort or time away. There is power in getting off-campus and going away for a brief time with others. Relationships can grow in powerful ways in a short time. Plan parish-wide retreats, then, to explore spiritual growth. The intent of such a gathering, held at least once a year, is to draw together members of the community who might not otherwise connect and to explore the power of their common life. Such gatherings should include opportunities for worship, engagement with scripture, honest discernment about what God is calling the community to do, and of course, good social connection. Develop a committee to work and pray in preparation for such a gathering, so that it can be a more engaging event.

Reasons for the seasons

Each of the liturgical seasons has something to teach about the journey of faith. Invite people to discern the significance of each season for their own spiritual development. Both Lent and Advent are especially appropriate times to ask questions like: Where am I in my relationship with God, myself, other people, and the world around me? In what areas do I have the greatest opportunity to learn and grow? What steps will I take in the next six to nine months to renew and strengthen that aspect of my spiritual life? With whom will I share this plan and ask them to help me be accountable for this growth? Taking advantage of the church calendar in this way provides an opportunity for sustained reflection on spiritual health and vitality.

Technology as an instrument of the gospel

During the COVID-19 pandemic, the church was forced to rely on technology and social media in new ways. While in one sense, online gathering increased a sense of longing and loss about being together, it also taught us that technological resources can get people moving in spiritual growth. As we witnessed around the world, people who had never participated in the Daily Office suddenly discovered it to be a sustaining spiritual resource that helped them grow in a challenging season. Churches that had never entertained the thought of streaming services or allowing cameras and screens in their sacred spaces now employ such tools to bring the community together. Getting people moving, then, means an openness on the part of leaders and their congregations to make use of all available resources.

Is this all about programming?

In short, no. Getting people moving is as much about culture change as it is about programming, budgets, and staff meetings. Be careful not to start a bunch of new ministries that only exhaust the leader and the congregation. Vital congregations actually do fewer things better. Examples of culture change include a commitment to begin every church meeting and ministry with prayer. That shift in spiritual culture does not change what the church is doing, but rather it changes the perspective to see that all we do in the church can be an opportunity for deepening relationships with God and others. One church, for instance, approached the tiresome project of cleaning the church basement by beginning and ending the workday with prayer, transforming the task into ministry and making a grim task valuable and holy. Another church ran a fundraising fair for years, with proceeds benefiting local outreach efforts. On the day of the fair, they gathered all the volunteers for prayer in the church, asking God for blessing on the efforts that day and for all those who would be assisted by those efforts. Such attention helped to form a culture of spiritual growth.

Getting people moving entails action—but merely increasing the number of activities does not necessarily inspire greater spiritual growth. Rather, getting people moving is about forming communities singularly committed to a deeper relationship with God and growing in love of God and neighbor. As noted, this may be as simple as beginning and ending each meeting with prayer, or welcoming newcomers with an expectation of spiritual growth, or weaving scripture into all that happens in the church (which we explore in the next chapter). Regardless of how we get people moving, however, such movement involves living into the grace that God extends to each one of us. When people get moving, God is at work. And that's a wonder to behold.

Questions
for Reflection

As you think about your congregation, is it more like a club for folks who have imagined they've arrived or a school for disciples who are on the way?

In your own spiritual journey, what were the things that got you moving? What got in the way?

Are growth and transformation expectations for members of your congregation?

4

Embed Scripture
in Everything

What happens when Episcopalians read the Bible? One church got wind of the news that engagement with scripture could be transformative so they decided they would read through the Bible in a year. Not every single word, mind you, but from September to May they would read and discuss key stories, moving from Genesis to Revelation and getting a sense of the overall trajectory. The congregation was excited; they embraced the challenge. Many had not cracked open a Bible since confirmation or a college survey course on religion. In their small town, people heard about this. One day the rector went to retrieve the morning local paper, and the headline read: "Episcopalians Read the Bible." Apparently, that was newsworthy! Biblical literacy is not always the first thing people associate with Episcopal culture.

Consider the testimony of Marek Zabriskie, rector of Christ Church in Greenwich, Connecticut, and founder of the Bible Challenge:

> Studies show that scripture is the number one spiritual tool for
> creating stronger Christian lives.... You cannot do something
> once a month and hope to make significant progress whether
> it's going to the gym, studying a foreign language, dieting
> or quitting smoking. Hence, this is no strategy for teaching

scripture to our people.... The best way that I know to create strong, committed, articulate and contagious Christians is to embed scripture in everything that we do and encourage all our members to engage in a daily spiritual practice of prayerful Bible reading.

Our research reinforces Zabriskie's claim: engagement with scripture is indeed one of the most effective catalysts for spiritual growth in congregations. At every stage along the spiritual continuum, engagement with scripture makes a difference. When we tell Episcopalians these findings, we are sometimes met with suspicion. Often, people tell us that Bible reading is for evangelicals or fundamentalists, biblical literalists who want to check their brains at the door, science-deniers who have nothing to do with the Anglican tradition. But if we can move past these presumptions, we find a great opportunity to help people grow spiritually through engagement with scripture. We can find supporting evidence for that assertion by looking at our own tradition and our own biblical heritage.

❖ What Does Scripture Say About Scripture?

It may be helpful to begin this discussion by recognizing the ways sacred text has shaped the community throughout the history. It may seem circular to explore what scripture says about scripture. But from start to finish, people of faith have been guided and transformed by attentiveness to sacred text. In Deuteronomy (6:5-9), Moses gives instructions to the children of Israel who have wandered in the wilderness and are on the cusp of entering the promised land. He instructs them that the word is very near them, that they are to write it on their hearts. It is meant to be part of everyday life. They should talk with their children about it when they are home or when they are away, when they lie down and rise up. They are to put those sacred words as a sign on their hand, on their forehead. Write them on the doorposts of their houses. In short, they are to embed the words of scripture in everything they do. As the children of Israel cross the Jordan into the promised land, Joshua, their new leader, challenges them by saying that the book of the law shall not depart from them. They are to meditate on it day and night (Joshua 1:8-9).

In the longest of the psalms, Psalm 119, every single verse (all 176 of them) contends that the law (also referred to as statutes or commandments or teaching of God) provides a guide. This psalm tells us that God's word is a lantern to our feet. When Israel needs reformation after a series of kings who have forsaken the tradition, King Josiah finds a copy of the law hidden in a closet (2 Kings 22). He reads it, takes it to heart, repents of the ways the people have gotten off track, and uses the recovered sacred text as guide to bring the people back into relationship with God. Years later, when those same people return from exile, they gather for the reading of the word (Nehemiah 8). The word guides them in rebuilding their city, a comforting and relevant thought as we consider the church these days in need of reform and rebuilding.

In the New Testament, we see that Jesus knows his scriptures, that he came to fulfill those scriptures, not abolish them (Matthew 5:17). We'll talk more about the distinctive way Jesus read scripture, but it is clear the text serves as guide for him. The gospel writers make the point that in his life and ministry, Jesus fulfills what has been written, making repeated reference to texts from what we now call the Old Testament. Saint Paul also writes about the nature of scripture: "All scripture is inspired by God and is useful for teaching, for reproof, for correction, and for training in righteousness, so that everyone who belongs to God may be proficient, equipped for every good work" (2 Timothy 3:16-17).

❖ What Does Tradition Say About Scripture?

Our liturgy underscores the importance of scripture as guide. It is interesting to note that when Episcopalians begin to dive into the Bible, they often express surprise at how much of the Bible seems to be lifted from the prayer book. Of course, it's the other way around, as those who crafted prayer books recognized the spiritual power inherent in scripture. Our prayer book finds scripture embedded in its pages, built on the premise of the following collect (prayer), which we read once a year.

> Blessed Lord, who caused all holy Scriptures to be written for our learning: Grant us so to hear them, read, mark, learn, and inwardly digest them, that we may embrace and ever hold fast the blessed hope of everlasting life, which you have given us in our Savior Jesus Christ; who lives and reigns with you and the Holy Spirit, one God, for ever and ever. *Amen.*

> —The Book of Common Prayer, p. 236

This collect speaks about the importance of scripture as a source of learning and hope. It provides a wonderful guide to study of scripture, as it moves deeper and deeper into our hearts so that it is eventually inwardly digested, becoming part of who we are and the journey on which we are headed.

In the prayer book, we find several lectionaries (or schedules of Bible readings) that invite us to read all parts of scripture, not just the ones that we like or ones that confirm our theological predispositions. Preachers are called to use those lectionaries as a guide. On a given Sunday, those who attend worship will hear lots of scripture, perhaps even more than in other churches that claim to be "Bible-based" or "Bible-centered."

Upon ordination in the Episcopal Church, clergy make a pledge regarding their view of scripture. Consider this exchange between the bishop and the ordinand:

Q: Will you be loyal to the doctrine, discipline, and worship of Christ as this Church has received them? And will you, in accordance with the canons of this Church, obey your bishop and other ministers who may have authority over you and your work?

A: I am willing and ready to do so; and I solemnly declare that I do believe the Holy Scriptures of the Old and New Testaments to be the Word of God, and to contain all things necessary to salvation; and I do solemnly engage to conform to the doctrine, discipline, and worship of the Episcopal Church.

—The Book of Common Prayer, p. 526

Note that the ordinand claims that scripture is the Word of God containing all that is necessary for salvation. He or she does not claim infallibility or inerrancy. This is not a pledge to biblical literalism or a fundamentalist approach to the text. It is not worship of the Bible itself. It is an affirmation that the scripture contains what is needed for salvation, for deliverance, for healing, for wholeness, all making a good argument for embedding scripture in the life of the community.

In the Outline of the Faith in the Prayer Book (also known as the Catechism), we find a series of questions on page 853 about the role of scripture in the life of the community:

Q: What are the Holy Scriptures?

A: The Holy Scriptures, commonly called the Bible, are the books of the Old and New Testaments; other books, called the Apocrypha, are often included in the Bible.

Q: What is the Old Testament?

A: The Old Testament consists of books written by the people of the Old Covenant, under the inspiration of the Holy Spirit, to show God at work in nature and history.

Q: What is the New Testament?

A: The New Testament consists of books written by the people of the New Covenant, under the inspiration of the Holy Spirit, to set forth the life and teachings of Jesus and to proclaim the Good News of the Kingdom for all people.

Q: Why do we call the Holy Scriptures the Word of God?

A: We call them the Word of God because God inspired their human authors and because God still speaks to us through the Bible.

Q: How do we understand the meaning of the Bible?

A: We understand the meaning of the Bible by the help of the Holy Spirit, who guides the Church in the true interpretation of the Scriptures.

All of these elements reinforce the importance of scripture in our tradition. But what difference does it make in the life of the church these days? United Methodist Bishop William H. Willimon—who now serves as professor of the practice of Christian ministry and director of the Doctor of Ministry program at Duke Divinity School—describes an encounter with a neighbor who asked about church. The neighbor said his preacher was always encouraging congregants to invite someone to church. The neighbor wasn't sure why she would invite someone to be part of church. She didn't see the difference between church and other gatherings. In terms of friendliness and caring, she got that at Rotary Club, which at least met at a convenient time in the week. As for racial inclusivity, the Durham Bulls did a better job than any church she'd attended. So, she asked the bishop: "What makes the church different?" Willimon ventured this response:

A congregation is Christian to the degree that it is confronted by and attempts to form its life in response to the Word of God. As Christians, we are people of a book. In our life with the Bible, we claim to have been confronted by the living Lord.... That divine/human dialogue is the originating event of the church. If the church fails to be a people of the Bible, then it might as well stop meeting on Sunday mornings and meet instead for lunch on Wednesdays, like any other well-intentioned civic club.

❖ How Can Leaders Embed Scripture in Everything the Church Does?

Spiritual leaders play a central role in establishing a scripturally engaged congregation. As noted earlier, spiritual leaders in the Anglican tradition commit to scripture as the Word of God, as we heard in the ordination service, containing all things necessary for salvation. Twentieth-century theologian Karl Barth is often credited with saying that preachers should have the Bible in one hand and the newspaper in the other. The role then for the spiritual leader, who serves as preacher, teacher, counselor, interpreter of scripture, is to take ancient texts and apply them to the contemporary spiritual journey—to the lives of individuals and to the lives of communities.

Of course, it's not always easy to translate the biblical voice to congregants who have mixed levels of trust, experience, and confidence in reading (and interpreting) the Bible. Add to that the difficulty of speaking publicly on scripture amid growing distrust of religious institutions and suspicion toward how scripture is used (and misused) politically. Based on our research of spiritually vital churches, however, several key strategies appear to make the work of transition and translation possible for spiritual leaders.

Leaders must believe that the scripture is worth studying

Recalling what we said in a previous chapter about the heart of the leader, it's important for rectors and other leaders (clergy and lay) to actively work on their own discipleship. We cannot assume that is happening. Reading and reflecting on scripture on a regular basis—and not simply in preparation for Sunday worship—are important ways leaders can live into the transformative power of scripture. If scripture is shaping the leader's individual spiritual journey, that person is better able to call the community to a similar kind of engagement.

Leaders embrace their role as teachers

A number of best practice churches lean toward the expository-teaching style. They look for opportunities in preaching and in class settings to go deep into the scripture, with exegesis that explains the context of the passage and its meaning for the community for whom it was written. From that, they are able to explore the "so-what" factor: How does this piece of scripture apply to life, Monday through Saturday? What difference does it make? Their starting point is the scripture, followed by application to the world in which congregants live.

Leaders take away the excuses for not reading the Bible

When congregants say they don't have time, or scripture is too hard to understand, or scripture is not relevant, leaders address each of those objections. Best practice churches make Bible engagement practical, meaningful, and accessible—something that can fit the busiest of schedules. Everybody can find some way to engage with scripture on a daily basis, even if it is just spending a few minutes. We'll consider some practical ways to foster that engagement later in the second half of this chapter.

Leaders model scripture as the church's foundation

Everywhere you turn in best practice churches, the Bible is embedded in the life of the church and its leadership. This includes everything from worship to serving experiences to leadership selection and training. Every ministry activity includes biblical guidance and inspiration. Inevitably, leaders will hear objections to the reading of scripture, for all kinds of reasons. If they're not hearing objections, they're probably not offering enough challenge.

Consider a case study of how one leader focuses on the role of scripture in preparation for preaching. The Sunday sermon, after all, is for many parishioners their primary engagement with scripture. Conn, the rector of Seattle's Church of the Epiphany, has developed a process for sharing his sermon preparation with the congregation, even adapting it for sermons delivered via streaming rather than live on Sunday mornings.

On Tuesday mornings, he meets with a sermon review team, consisting of clergy, music director, lay leader/editor, communications minister, and a different parishioner each week. The first fifteen minutes of this meeting are spent reviewing the in-person and recorded sermon from the previous Sunday, and then they complete the following steps over several days:

1. They spend time in Bible study on the lectionary selections for the Sunday twelve days hence.

2. They ask the scheduled preacher to name something in the text that particularly inspires passion or curiosity.

3. The group considers what is going on in the church, liturgically, programmatically, or socially.

4. They consider what is going on in the world (again, the Bible in one hand, the newspaper in the other).

The next day (Wednesday), the preacher writes a draft of the sermon. On Thursday and Friday, the preacher continues to work and refine the draft, and, when ready, forwards it to the lay editor. Over the course of the next few days, the preacher and editor share edits back and forth as necessary. On the following Tuesday or Wednesday, the preacher practices the sermon in the pulpit. On Thursday, the preacher pre-records the sermon for the coming Sunday. Finally, on Sunday, the preacher sends the written sermon to the communications minister to be posted online and offers the sermon to the congregation. On the next Tuesday, there is one more opportunity to review.

This process may not work for every congregation. But it offers a model for those who wish to honor the importance of the sermon in the life of the community. It shows a way to make the sermon the most excellent and relevant offering possible. When leadership pays this kind of attention to the sermon, members of the congregation will pay attention as well.

❖ Does It Matter How We Read Scripture?

Scripture has power. What will we do with that power? How will we be stewards of that life-giving word in ways that build people up rather than divide or diminish them?

A pastor was asked to preside at the wedding of a young couple, both of whom were graduate students at a fine university. The groom was son of a lay leader in the church. The bride was an avowed atheist, but she was graciously willing to have a religious service to honor her new in-laws. It didn't hurt that the wedding was scheduled to take place in a beautiful and grand church.

Premarital counseling sessions with this couple went well beyond issues of relationships in marriage. The clergy and couple had extended conversation about the faith, questions about the ability to reconcile science and technology with religion, and confession of the ways that the church had wounded this young couple. At the conclusion of the sessions, the couple expressed their appreciation for the pastor and his willingness to engage their questions. They even gave him a book, *The Bible Tells Me So: The Uses and Abuses of Scripture.* A scan of the table of contents explains the point of the book. There's a chapter on how the Bible was used to support slavery, followed by a chapter on how the Bible supported the case of abolitionists. There was a chapter on how the Bible forbade women's ordination, followed by a chapter on how the Bible could provide an argument for women's ordination. You get the idea. On the cover of the book, there was a quote from Shakespeare: "Even the devil can quote scripture." It's a reference to the story of Jesus's encounter with the devil in the wilderness, where they engage in dueling proof-texting (See Matthew 3 or Luke 4).

As we seek to embed scripture in the life of the community, leaders must recognize the ways it has been used to work against spiritual growth, against a deepening of love of God and neighbor. That is why we read scripture in light of tradition. That is why we read scripture in light of reason. That is why we read scripture in light of experience. That is why it is important we read scripture in community, in a way that welcomes questions and recognizes not only the usefulness but also the abuse that has been inflicted.

In *Jesus and the Disinherited*, theologian and civil rights leader Howard Thurman tells the story of visiting his grandmother, a woman of deep Christian faith who was born a slave and lived on a plantation until the Civil War. She could neither read nor write. Thurman was charged with reading the Bible to her a couple times a week. They read from all parts of the Bible except the letters of Paul, 1 Corinthians 13 exempted. When he was a college student, he asked his grandmother why she had not allowed the reading of Pauline letters. She said that during the days of slavery, the master's minister would occasionally hold services for those who were enslaved. The white minister used as his text something from Paul. At least three or four times a year, he used as a text: "Slaves, be obedient to them that are your masters... as unto Christ." Then he would go on to show how it was God's will that they all were slaves and how, if they were good and happy slaves, God would bless them. She said: "I promised my Maker that if I ever learned to read and if freedom ever came, I would not read that part of the Bible."

We can all cite examples of this kind of abuse and injustice. We can also find ways that engagement with scripture has worked for justice and peace. The reading of the Sermon on the Mount was transformative for Leo Tolstoy, who read the sermon and gave up much of his wealth, embracing a life of nonviolence. In turn, Mahatma Gandhi reflected on Tolstoy's interpretation of the Sermon on the Mount and embraced Jesus's teaching to shape his transformative movement of nonviolence on the Asian subcontinent. (It should be noted that Gandhi was often encouraged to convert to Christianity and apparently gave it some thought. But after an experience of racial discrimination in South Africa, he offered this searing critique of the church: "I like your Christ, but not your Christians. Your Christians are so unlike your Christ.") In turn, Martin Luther King Jr. adopted the wisdom of Tolstoy and Gandhi as they appropriated Jesus's teaching. King used their witness to guide the Civil Rights Movement in the United States, a movement toward beloved community, a movement in which those who participated in marches and other acts of nonviolent civil disobedience were given a Rule of Life that included daily prayer and daily reading of scripture.

As we speak of how we read scripture, we note that Jesus was steeped in his own tradition of reading scripture, yet he still brought his own interpretation to the sacred texts. Again and again, he violated the rules of the sabbath, clearly set forth in scripture, for a higher good, the healing of those who came to him. In the Sermon on the Mount, Jesus calls his disciples to a higher standard of love. He notes biblical injunctions against murder, against adultery, and then he raises the stakes. He begins by saying, for instance "You have heard that it was said you shall not commit murder." And then he continues, "But I say to you, if you are angry with your brother or sister, you have committed murder." In talking with his disciples, Jesus warns against idolatry of sacred text when he says in John 5:39, "You search the scriptures because you think that in them you have eternal life; and it is they that testify on my behalf."

Centuries later, author C. S. Lewis put his spin on this idea, contending that it is Christ himself, not the Bible, who is the true Word of God. The Bible, read in the right spirit and with the guidance of good teachers, will bring us to him.

It matters how we read scripture and how we allow the Word to contribute to our spiritual growth, that is, our growth in love of God and neighbor.

❖ What Are Some Practical Ways To Embed Scripture In Everything?

As part of our research, we have learned several approaches that congregations have taken to embed scripture into everything they do. Below are some examples.

Read the Bible together

Several years ago, Gunn, executive director of Forward Movement, was serving as rector of a church. He discovered the congregation was not particularly well read in the scriptures, so he implemented a program for the congregation to read the Bible together over the course of the year. He explains:

> We started the year by reading the whole Bible out loud one weekend. Then we proceeded to work our way through the whole Bible. We used a summary book for adults and another for children on Sundays. And we had a group that met on Thursday evenings who wanted to read every word on every page. It was transformational. For me, I saw the big picture

of scripture in ways I hadn't before this. And for the people in this church, they learned more about the breadth and depth of God's steadfast love. We learned to connect our own stories to the vast and amazing story of God's great love for us. Unrelated to scripture engagement specifically but connected to adult formation, we do have some data on giving. Our treasurer looked at pledging and matched pledge data to families who participated in adult formation offerings. Over a three-year period, in families where no adults took part in adult formation, their pledges went up about 4 percent on average. In families where at least one adult took part in a course, their pledge went up over 60 percent (in three years). Now this is only one church, but it's a pretty amazing bit of data. Anecdotally, I know that people who became more immersed in the scriptures attended church more regularly, were more eager to serve in ministries, and gave more generously.

Many churches of all denominations around the nation have used *The Story* published by Zondervan as the theme of yearlong education program for all ages, and they, like Gunn, discovered that the number of participants increased along with biblical literacy. Many Episcopal churches use *The Path*, a resource created by Forward Movement that presents the grand story of the Bible in a narrative fashion, using excerpts from the New Revised Standard Version. In congregations using these books, people are not only encouraged to read on their own but also to join small study groups that have emerged spontaneously in the course of study. Both resources offer materials for children and youth as well as adults. The Bible Challenge, the ministry founded and led by Marek Zabriskie (cited at the beginning of this chapter) also presents several ways to read scripture as a congregation over varying periods of time.

Daily devotionals

Another way to engage with scripture is to encourage daily reading. An example in the Episcopal tradition is the use of *Forward Day by Day,* an instrument in spiritual growth familiar to many Episcopalians. Derived from the lectionary found in the Book of Common Prayer, this daily devotional takes its cue from those scripture passages and invites readers to find their way in the Bible, out of the conviction that the Bible is relevant not only in church but in the home and workplace. There are many other resources for daily devotionals available online. Christ Church in Charlotte, North Carolina, for instance, simply sends out a single verse each morning. One need not be a member of that church to receive those daily emails, which are available for free.

Scriptural reflection in all church gatherings (even business meetings)

When a congregation commits to including scripture engagement in every meeting of the church, the practice is a tangible expression of the belief that scripture is central to deepening our relationship with God. Over time, this practice will shift the culture of a congregation to one deeply steeped in the Word of God. One vestry committed to begin its meetings with scripture reflection, led each month by a different vestry member. This action expressed the expectation that the Word of God would be incorporated in all the work (the business) of the church.

This type of culture shift reflects the belief intrinsic in the prayer we shared earlier, that every member of the church is capable of "reading, marking, and inwardly digesting scripture." While we recognize there will always be a wide range of interpretations of the meaning of the word of God, this practice of allowing groups to be "shaped by the Bible" helps differentiate the ministries of the church from all the other volunteer efforts with which people are involved.

Bibles in the pews

Another way to help embed scripture in the life of the congregation is to make sure there are Bibles in the pews. This step sounds simple, but many Episcopal churches only have hymnals and prayer books in their pews. The act of including a Bible is a visible reminder of its importance. We suggest not only placing Bibles in the pews but also using them during worship on Sundays. One rector challenged congregants to find the passages as they were read during worship. Another added in a listing of the page number in the Bible in the bulletin. For many, this is a most basic introduction, as one rector was heard to say: "Romans is to the right of Acts and to the left of 1 Corinthians." Don't be afraid to approach biblical literacy at the level of the lowest common denominator. Nothing is lost by being too explanatory. The neophytes will appreciate the help, and the more biblically literate will feel smart and self-satisfied.

Bible timeline

Don't take biblical literacy for granted. Many people—especially Episcopalians—have had limited interaction with the Bible. One way to address that is to create a Bible timeline. Eager to instruct congregants in the basic structure of the Bible, a small church in New Hampshire put up a long roll of white paper in the parish hall and invited parishioners to draw their favorite Bible stories and place them chronologically. The timeline stayed up for several months. Parishioners of all ages participated. As the number of drawings increased, interest in the biblical narrative did as well. To be sure, this type of approach could invite some heated discussions over chronology (which should go first: Paul's letters or the gospels?), but even this type of discussion can deepen a congregation's collective relationship to the scriptures.

The Good Book Club

For the past several years, Forward Movement has partnered with Episcopal organizations to sponsor the Good Book Club. The initiative invites Episcopalians to read a portion of scripture for an entire liturgical season, such as Epiphany, Lent, or Easter. The project grew out of research that indicates the transformative effect of scripture. During the season of Epiphany 2021, churches were invited to read the Gospel of Mark, and a schedule was set up to read a bit of scripture each day. Other resources like online classes and background material were offered. The results reflected other findings, with participants reporting increases in the importance of scripture and how it impacts their daily lives. A survey taken after the Good Book Club concluded for the Gospel of Mark also found:

- a 10 percent increase in daily reading of scripture—and a 4 percent decline in rarely reading
- more than double the familiarity of the stories of Mark and an increase in prayer life
- parishioners noted a significant growth in understanding of the gospel and a nearly unanimous desire to continue with additional sessions of the Good Book Club

Almost all the respondents were lay people, not clergy, and their response shows a hunger for scripture engagement. Congregations can implement their own Good Book Club, using materials from previous seasons or joining in the current session.

Preparing for Sunday

We read a lot of scripture on Sundays at church. Often, the excerpts of scripture provided by the lectionary leave people wondering about context. One of the ways to address that is to encourage congregants to spend time before Sunday reading the passages that will be part of the liturgy on Sunday.

Some parishes offer weekly Bible studies that focus on the scripture readings for the coming Sunday. These kinds of studies provide not only background on the gospel for the coming Sunday but also thoughtful questions for reflection. A good example is St. Stephen's Church in Richmond, Virginia, which convenes weekly Wednesday night study groups to explore the upcoming Sunday lectionary. This type of study not only deepens biblical literacy but also makes the experience of worship more engaging and helps build a sense of community as people grow together.

Verses posted around the church

St. John's Church in Memphis took the call to embed scripture quite literally. Visitors will notice that all over their rather large church campus, they have posted small and discrete laminated copies of verses, printed in an attractive font. So, for example, verses posted in the kitchen talk about how Jesus fed people. Near a light switch can be found a verse like "Your word is a lantern on my feet." By a water fountain might be found a biblical claim that Jesus gives living water.

Lay Bible studies

While our tradition rightly honors biblical scholarship, you don't have to be an expert to study the Bible. Small groups can meet in a variety of ways. Here are three examples of simple Bible study methods that are widely accessible to congregants, especially those who may not have studied the Bible before:

The African Bible Study Method: This method was introduced by the African delegation to the Lambeth Conference in 1998. This method is, therefore, known by both names: "Lambeth" and "African." It is similar to the practice of *lectio divina* (a reflective reading and praying of scripture). After an opening prayer, one person reads the passage slowly. Without discussion or explanation, each person identifies a word or phrase that catches their attention. Each person then shares the word or phrase around the group without discussion. Another person reads the passage slowly. In quiet reflection, each person identifies how this passage touches their life that day, then each person shares with the group. The passage is read a third time. Each person writes their answer to: "From what I've heard and shared, what do I believe God wants me to do or be? Is God inviting me to change in any way?" Each person shares their answer. Each person prays for the person on their right, naming what was shared in the other steps. Then the group closes with the Lord's Prayer and a couple moments of silence.

Equipping the Saints: Verna J. Dozier, a high school English teacher and a religious educator, focused adult education on Bible study and claiming the authority of the laity. She is credited by many in the Episcopal Church with changing the field of scripture study and refocusing attention on the ministry of all the baptized. After taking early retirement from public school education in 1975, she worked full-time as religious educator, church conference leader, consultant to church groups, and author of books and articles on the ministry of God's people in the world.

Dozier's career commenced with guidelines for studying the Bible. Her first published book was aptly entitled *Equipping the Saints: A Method of Self-directed Bible Study for Lay Groups* (1981). Her basic method involved three steps:

1.   Clarifying what the passage was saying: Are we all understanding what is going on in this passage?

2.   Clarifying why this passage was preserved: What does the scripture say to the people for whom it was written?

3.   Reflecting on what the passage means to its readers and to the church today: What difference does this passage make in my life?

Throughout her life, Dozier emphasized that laity, not just clergy, need to use critical biblical resources that allow for a multiple hearing of voices and not one translation or interpretation. She encouraged laity to believe that "they were accepted," insisted that God's love is "boundless," and advocated moving "from Sunday Christians to Monday Christians" at work in the world.

Dwelling in the Word: This process has been promoted by Zscheile, author of *People of the Way*. Here is a description of the process as used by the Diocese of Oxford and described by Patrick Keifert. He writes: "Dwelling in the word is deliberately not about sharing information or seeking scholarly answers or even the right answers to issues raised in the text. It is about listening each other into free speech and discerning what God is up to amongst us. It is often used at the beginning of a meeting and sets a powerful spiritual formation for the work of the gathering."

In this process, groups:

1. Start with prayer and invite the Holy Spirit to be a guide in the study of scripture.

2. Read the passage. Have different people read the stories at each meeting so all can participate. Then allow time for silent reflection.

3. Encourage people to find a discussion partner, ideally someone they do not know well. Invite the person to share what they heard in the passage and to answer two questions: What captured your imagination in the passage? What would you like to find out more about? Then, the second person takes a turn offering their answers. Both participants should listen well, because they will report back to the group their partner's answers.

When the larger group reconvenes, everyone shares their partner's responses. Then the group wrestles together with what God might be up to in the passage for that day.

Keifert cautions, "This discipline is far from magic. It's not guaranteed to solve all the problems or answer all questions that a council or committee must address. However, over time, this discipline forms a community where the Spirit is welcome and expected."

These three models indicate that there are many ways to engage with scripture. There are many other approaches, of course. Leaders may want to develop their own and/or concoct their own combination of multiple approaches.

Leaders play a key role in embedding scripture into everything a congregation does. But it is also the case that each person bears both the freedom and the responsibility to deepen their own spiritual life. We've repeatedly offered the metaphor of exercise, imagining the church as spiritual gym. As in all areas of health, how we nurture that health matters.

Questions
for Reflection

What are the ways that scripture is part of the life of your congregation? Apart from the lectionary offerings in Sunday worship, how is scripture read in your church?

How do you and members of your congregation deal with difficult passages?

If you are a leader of a congregation, how does engagement with scripture inform your ministry?

What is one new way you might embed scripture in the life of your community?

5

Create Ownership

The pastor loved his congregation. He had spent years alongside them, marrying and burying and countless meetings in between. But on one Sunday, he seemed a bit frustrated. He had embraced the idea that engagement with scripture was key to spiritual growth in a Christian community but wasn't convinced that congregants were ever actually picking up the Good Book themselves. So, with a measure of exasperation, he approached the pulpit and told the congregation: "I can't read the Bible for you."

No matter how many scripture readings he recited or expository sermons he delivered, this pastor could not serve as a substitute for the personal transformation that comes with reading the Bible for oneself. This is what we mean by creating a sense of ownership. Just as individuals must actively participate in their own spiritual journeys, so too must everyone play their part in the spiritual life of their faith community. The Jesus Movement is not a spectator sport; we must get everyone onto the field.

At the same time, however, a fundamental component of the Christian faith is belief in a theology of grace, and this notion is central to vital communities. There is nothing we can do to earn God's love—or, as author Rob Bell has said, there's nothing we can do to make God love us less. Creating a sense of ownership is not about earning God's favor but rather a matter of recognizing that in the life of faith—a life that, at its core, is a relationship—we are called to participate, to do our part to deepen that relationship with God.

❖ What Does Scripture Say About Creating Ownership?

While the particular words "create ownership" don't appear in holy writ, the principle is at work. As we've already noted, our faith rests on God's amazing grace. That's stated beautifully in Ephesians 2:8-10, which says that by grace we have been saved through faith. It is a gift, not a measure of merit, lest anyone should boast. But with that foundation of God's love, the author of the letter says that we, as God's creative work, are created for good works that God prepared beforehand to be our way of life. Another translation renders it: God has made good works for us to walk in. The willingness, indeed, the commitment to walk into those good works, is at the heart of creating ownership.

The image of walking in those good works can be traced back to the children of Israel in Exodus, an illustration of spiritual growth on the move. Their arrival at the borders of the promised land was nothing but gift. But in several sermons attributed to Moses in the book of Deuteronomy, we find a strong presentation of both the freedom and the responsibility that lies before them. In those sermons, the children of Israel are instructed in the way to live. The law presented in Torah is described as *haggadah* and *hallakah*, derived from verbs on how we walk and how we talk. The people of Israel are called daily to recite the *Shema*, an affirmation of loving both God and neighbor. Moses tells the people that God has set before them life and death, blessing and curse, and they are to choose life. They have agency in this process, and it matters what they do with it.

Centuries later, the prophets challenge the people of Israel—before they are in exile, while they are in exile, and after they come back from exile. Even in the depths of exile, when they would have felt most powerless and unable to effect change, the prophets call them to action. Micah famously speaks of what the Lord requires: To do justice. To love mercy. To walk humbly with God. That is every person's call, every person's responsibility.

Moving to the gospels, we notice that although Jesus doesn't use the language of "creating ownership," he does have expectations of spiritual growth in those whom he encounters. When a rich young ruler comes and asks what he must do to inherit eternal life, Jesus throws the question back on him, asking him to take a hard look at his affection for his possessions. It is up to this young man to take the steps to follow Jesus, but he declines. Jesus meets with another wealthy figure, Zacchaeus, who is converted to a better way of life over lunch. At the end of that encounter, Zacchaeus takes ownership, takes responsibility by making amends for the wrongs he has done, and gives away half of his wealth to feed the poor. Jesus meets the woman at the well, as described in John 4. He tells her everything she has ever done. Then he tells her to go and sin no more, to take charge of her life. In these and other encounters, Jesus meets people, often outsiders, with extravagant grace, and then he challenges them to walk into the new and abundant life God has for them.

In his teachings, most often to his small group of disciples, Jesus repeatedly raises the bar, elevating expectations. Those who wish to follow him are called to take up the cross and follow him. They will find their lives, oddly enough, by losing their lives. Many followers find his expectations too high and drift away. For those who stay, the cost is great, but it is outweighed by the promise. Centuries later, we are beneficiaries of the ways that they embraced ownership—not only of their own spiritual journeys but the health and vitality of their communities of faith as well.

As we move to Paul's letters, a theology of grace pervades. Again, scripture sets the stage for us to walk into a new life. In the letter to the Romans, Paul's most expansive articulation of his theology, he devotes the first eleven chapters to describing the mystery of God's gracious plans for all people: while we were yet sinners, Christ died for us. But the latter part of that letter describes the "so-what factor" of our lives in response to that grace. Chapter 12 begins with Paul saying, "I appeal to you, therefore, by the mercies of God, to present yourselves a living sacrifice." He invites his readers to be transformed and to take part in that process. The balance of his letter to the Romans offers guidance, coaching as to how to live faithfully in the world, each person with their own responsibility, each person taking their part in the body of Christ, each person exercising their gifts.

In the letter to the Philippians, Paul invites the congregation to work out their own salvation with fear and trembling, claiming in marvelous synergy that it is God who is at work in them to will and to do of his good pleasure. While coaching the early church, Paul often uses the metaphors of an athlete in training, a farmer patiently tilling the field, or a person in the military training. Everyone has a part.

That participation is captured in the first letter of Peter (4:10-11), which reads: "Like good stewards of the manifold grace of God, serve one another with whatever gift each of you has received. Whoever speaks must do so as one speaking the very words of God; whoever serves must do so with the strength that God supplies, so that God may be glorified in all things through Jesus Christ."

❖ What Does Our Liturgy Say About Creating Ownership?

Baptism is a good place to begin. Every time a church offers the sacrament of baptism as part of its public worship, it deepens a sense of ownership for the whole community. During that liturgy, the whole congregation reaffirms their baptismal vows, answering the five promises of the baptismal covenant in the first person: "I will with God's help." This is a powerful example of ownership coupled with divine grace.

Even if the words may become rote, even to clergy, the repetition of this covenant shapes a culture of ownership.

During the eucharist, each individual is invited to step out of the pew as able and come forward to receive the bread and wine. These elements are strength for the journey ahead. The eucharist then concludes with a prayer that we be sent into the world to love and serve the Lord with gladness and singleness of heart. These words suggest ownership, while also leaving it up to each person to figure out what that looks like.

In the Outline of the Faith (the Catechism), all members of the church have a role, beginning with a description of the laity. Each order in the church (bishops, priests, deacons, and lay persons) share the same ministry, which is to represent Christ. Much to the surprise of many, this is not only the job of clergy. All Christians are "professional" Christians; we all show Christ to the world.

The prayer book abounds with opportunities for growth in the spiritual life, and we will identify some of those later in this chapter. But, like the pastor who challenged his congregation by refusing to read the Bible for them, the riches of the prayer book are only savored if everyone shares in its wealth.

❖ How Can a Congregation Create a Sense of Ownership?

Creating ownership often demands a change in church culture, which may entail elevating expectations for members of the congregation. This usually begins with the ways we worship, since worship is at the heart of all we do. The Danish philosopher Søren Kierkegaard compared the liturgy to a dramatic performance. In his vision, clergy and musicians are prompters, members of the congregation are the actors, and God is the audience. While it may be an incomplete metaphor, making God seem passive, Kierkegaard's point is important. Members of the congregation do not come to church merely to see a performance, to decide whether the sermon and music is pleasing. Church is not a spectator sport nor is it a consumer product. Rather, we must challenge people to come with a sense of participation, responsibility, and ownership.

In recent years, attendance at weekly worship has markedly declined. Clergy, for the most part, have little interest in acting as truant officers, monitoring who shows up and who does not. But members of the clergy do have a responsibility to challenge congregants to be present.

One element of creating ownership has to do with simply showing up, which the comedian Groucho Marx described as 95 percent of life. This is not, of course, because clergy want to deprive parishioners of a Sunday morning with the newspaper or an early tee time at the golf course. From the beginning of the church, Christians gathered for weekly worship—specifically on Sundays in celebration of Christ's resurrection—and especially for regular spiritual nourishment from the eucharist. This weekly attendance provides sustenance for individuals, and it brings the community together for a common meal. It matters whether people show up. Loaves and fishes mold and spoil without a crowd to enjoy them.

❖ How Can Leaders Encourage a Sense Of Ownership?

Not surprisingly, leadership is key in the process of creating ownership. We spoke earlier about how clergy are called to take steps to deepen their own spiritual lives. If that kind of spiritual work is not taking place, if it is not evident to the congregation, then it will be difficult to convince congregants to do that work as well. Once that basis is established, leaders are better able to establish an expectation that every individual in the community will grow in relationship with God, and with God's church, in their personal spiritual practice and in service.

A starting point for clergy leaders is to begin with lay leadership, articulating the expectation that everyone in leadership roles is meant to grow in their own spiritual lives. That often begins with the vestry (or parallel bodies in other denominations). The first step in this process is defining the vestry as a spiritual community as well as a governing board. One way to do this is by setting aside a vestry meeting (or a portion of an annual vestry retreat) for members to share spiritual autobiographies and offer personal plans for spiritual growth. Another possibility is to establish vestry prayer partners so that each member is praying for another member and their spiritual goals throughout the year. After all, a group offering leadership in a church should look different than leadership in other kinds of governing bodies in other organizations. Why not celebrate that?

Bonnie Perry, who now serves as bishop of Michigan, served for 25 years as rector of All Saints Church in Chicago. Under her leadership, a small and struggling congregation transformed into an amazingly vital church with spiritual depth and compelling outreach. Early on in her ministry, she set a high bar for participation on the vestry. In their monthly meetings, they spent the first hour of their time together in Bible study and prayer for one another. Of course, that meant their monthly meetings might last for two and a half hours. But she told prospective vestry members upfront that if they wished to serve on vestry, Bible study and prayer were part of the deal. She elevated expectations, and it transformed her community.

But what about those who aren't leaders?

When it comes to inspiring and equipping people to take ownership of their own spiritual growth, the natural inclination for church leaders (clergy and lay) is to rely on traditional levers, such as volunteer programs, small groups, and training for lay leaders who lead programs. Best practice churches take advantage of all these levers. But the goal is not simply to build up programs. More church activity does not necessarily mean increased spiritual growth. Often, more activity just tires people out, so that they can't wait to be relieved of church duty. The goal is to change behavior—and that kind of change, again, involves elevating expectations. Before getting into specific programs or activities that can spur a sense of ownership, there are several ways to approach this culture shift.

It begins with empowering people to be the church outside of church. Our experience with the COVID-19 pandemic helped people realize that the church is more than its buildings. In many ways, the isolation brought on by the pandemic increased an appreciation for inspiring architecture and the healing power of sacred space. But it also allowed people to realize that church is ultimately about people. In such challenging times, people learned that they must be intentional about finding ways to be in relationship with God and neighbor.

In the Christian tradition, this understanding has been referred to as the "priesthood of all believers," that is, the flattening out of clergy-lay distinctions so that all Christians recognize their "priestly" function. Brian McLaren expressed this in a piece entitled "Everyone Is Clergy: A Liturgical Reading."

> Everyone is clergy. Everyone is called to serve,
> To create, to communicate,
> To participate with our good Creator
> In the making and remaking of our good world.
> Everyone is clergy. Everyone is called to stand,
> To struggle, to suffer, to trust and to love,
> And so to join in the unmaking of injustice and
> In the liberation of earth from every form of sin.
> Everyone is clergy. Everyone is called to holiness,
> To faithfulness, to health, to growth,
> To serenity and activity,
> To the practices of life
> In the kingdom of God.
> All our daily work is holy. Every act of service,
> Every deed of neighborly kindness,

Create Ownership

Every smile or sigh, every touch or tear
Can be a sacramental act expressing the presence of the
living God.
Every drop of sweat that falls in honest labor for the
common good
Joins with every movement toward others
In the daily liturgy of human work.
Some are given special gifts to equip and inspire others
for this daily work of faith
And labor of love.
All are channels of grace, given, received,
Shared in a symphony of many voices and instruments,
So the earth may be filled with the glory of God.
You are clergy. So am I. Together
We are called to learn God's music of life
In the unique instruments of our bodies, our persons, our
times, our settings.
Then we are sent out to play it with joy and sincerity
wherever we go.
Together we are part of a truly apostolic succession:
The people of God sent into the world, generation after
generation,
As Jesus was sent by the Father,
In the power of the Holy Spirit,
For the good of the world.
So let us work and rest together,
Let us play and sing together,
Let us by our faithful lives bring glory to the true and
living God.
For we are all clergy
And we are all called.[1]

Brian D. McLaren, "Everyone Is Clergy," September 3, 2007, https://brianmclaren.
net/everyone-is-clergy/. Used with permission.

Shifting this mindset that divides clergy and congregants entails a significant culture change. Blurring those dividing lines involves assigning high levels of ministry accountability to lay leaders and using creative ways to inspire people to explore Christ-like behavior in their everyday lives.

The culture change also means equipping people to succeed. It's not enough to simply empower people. Lovingly establishing high standards for performance and accountability is critical, as is educating congregants and giving them tools they need to meet those standards. That's where good coaching comes in. That culture change means holding people accountable. Churches that apply this best practice principle of creating ownership understand that their attendees need spiritual mirrors. They need safe, relational networks to help them navigate the ups and downs of the journey of faith. Many invest significant time and resources in small-group infrastructures to provide that support. People who sense the need for these kinds of networks may need to go out of their way to find them.

❖ What Are Some Practical Ways to Create Ownership Within a Congregation?

Creating a sense of ownership is in many ways up to the individual. Each person in the church is endowed with both freedom and responsibility to deepen a relationship with God. At the same time, congregational leaders can facilitate that process, serving as coaches for people who are looking for ways to grow in faith.

Develop spiritual paths

This may mean articulating a Rule of Life for the parish. A Rule of Life is simply an agreed-upon set of standards or guidelines for behavior

Create Ownership

and spiritual practices. For instance, a Rule of Life may include a commitment to starting and ending all meetings in prayer. Of course, this agreement need not be called a "Rule of Life," if that language scares people off. And it need not be complicated or onerous. For example, Christ Church in Winnetka, Illinois, developed a "rule" that became a mark of identity for the community. The rule had four planks, for which I will provide brief commentary:

- *WORSHIP more than you don't.* In this community, many people traveled on weekends, and regular attendance at church was being redefined. Instead of laying on a guilt trip, leadership invited people to come together as often as possible, teaching about the importance of presence.
- *SEEK a deeper understanding of the faith.* If churches are in the business of making disciples, that means we are all students, all learners. Wherever people may find themselves in the spiritual journey, there is always a next step, always a way to go deeper.
- *SERVE others in the name and manner of Jesus.* Jesus teaches that if people want to meet him, they can do so in service. Each congregant is invited to find ways to serve others. Opportunities abound.
- *GIVE as generously as God has given to you.* This simple but profound statement proclaims that ownership is not about hoarding but rather about living into Jesus's counterintuitive statement that we find life by giving it away.

As discussed earlier, Presiding Bishop Curry has called upon the people of the Episcopal Church to embrace the Way of Love, seven verbs that describe a life of discipleship. These simple verbs provide a pathway for people to grow in faith.

- *Turn.* This is a somewhat gentler way to talk about repentance. It's about taking stock of the direction in which we are headed spiritually.

- *Learn.* Another word for disciple is student or learner. This applies especially to learning about scripture, a growth edge for many Episcopalians.
- *Pray.* This skill can be learned. It gets easier and grows in meaning with practice. It's about deepening a relationship with God.
- *Worship.* In whatever way we worship, it is about offering our best to God.
- *Bless.* It's a calling to go out into the world and bless those we meet in God's name.
- *Go.* Specifically, we are called to go and make disciples. It's related to blessing, and it means moving beyond the walls of the church, not expecting people to come to us but seeing what God is already up to in the neighborhood.
- *Rest.* If the Lord rested after six days of creation, we, too, can grow by taking sabbath, in whatever way that makes sense for our lives.

Living into these seven verbs provides a powerful way to create a sense of ownership in the spiritual journey.

Daily devotional time

Emphasize the importance of praying each day, maybe even several times a day. Encourage congregants to set an intention for this—with a specific time and perhaps in a specific chair. Invite people to set a timer on their phone. Perhaps suggest the 10/10 rule: ten minutes of prayer or silence and ten minutes of scripture reading. The prayer book is filled with helpful ways to observe daily worship. Certainly, the Daily Office, with prayers for morning, noon, evening, and end of day, is useful (starting on page 35 in the Book of Common Prayer). Of course, that can be a bit much for some, so we recommend as an alternative the Daily Devotions for Families and Individuals, which start on page 102 and take about ten to fifteen minutes and is an accessible way to weave prayer into daily life.

Parish prayer

Consider crafting a prayer for the parish that everyone knows and embraces. One parish in Memphis, Tennessee, did this. The prayer was offered before sermons, at all the business meetings of the church, and before service projects began. Over time, parishioners of all ages came to memorize it and say it together. It even carried over into other areas of life. It became a mark of the community and helped congregants realize that clergy were not—should not be— the only ones who did the praying. You can find this prayer in the appendix.

Congregational retreat

When people talk about times of spiritual growth, they often say this occurred during some kind of retreat, a weekend away with the church or some other similar event. These can be mountaintop experiences, sustaining people in the days and weeks that follow. They provide an excellent venue for people to focus on their own spiritual journey and then share their faith story with others. Such events can involve as many people as possible in the planning so that a wide group of people have ownership.

Identifying spiritual gifts

Consider offering discernment courses for people to identify their spiritual gifts. One church offered a course called, "What in God's Name Are You Doing?" The program used traditional practices associated with discernment to help people identify their vocations. This included more than just the work for which they get paid but also volunteer activities, life in their families, relationships with friends, and ministries in the church. Scripture, prayer, and the counsel of others in the community all emerge as ways to discover meaningful ministry. Some small groups have also used the book *Listening Hearts* as the basis for such discernment, in the recognition that all members of the church have a call.

There are also all kinds of online inventories that people can take. Of course, they vary in quality and theological perspective. One we recommend was crafted by Claire Woodley, a canon for ministry in the Diocese of Long Island. She says her ministry radically changed after reading *Listening Hearts* and Charles V. Bryant's *Rediscovering Your Spiritual Gifts*. "When I began to step intentionally into activity that engaged my spiritual giftedness, it was like stepping though a door and experiencing a different life; the power of God moving through my body, in my mind, my prayers, my preaching, and teaching. I can't imagine living without that joy and power now." She finds that the best spiritual gifts inventories are rooted in scripture, the sacraments, and the Holy Spirit.

An expansive view of the sermon

The pulpit has been described as that piece of furniture sitting six feet above contradiction. In some ways, it can be an outdated form of communication, providing no way for people to offer feedback, so it may be helpful occasionally to offer a more interactive alternative. This doesn't work in every church, of course, but you might experiment with ways to deepen engagement when it comes to the sermon. In one church, parishioners are encouraged to read appointed passages ahead of time and contemplate questions like: If I wrote this passage, what would be the headline? Where does the passage touch my life? How is God inviting me to change? Another church devised an approach to one of its weekend services by giving parishioners the opportunity to respond to the sermon. That is, the preacher offers the homily, and then three standing microphones are made available for people to come forward and offer their responses, whether questions or comments.

Another way to do this is to offer a forum after the sermon for people to discuss, ask questions of the preacher, and offer alternative interpretations. After all, the baptismal covenant tells us that we are all preachers—that is, we are to proclaim the good news in word and example.

Mentoring

Consider systematic ways to develop mentoring relationships within the parish. All kinds of ministries can forge deeper relationships within the church by inviting those who are new to the ministry to partner with those who have done the ministry for a while. One parish, for instance, has done this to welcome new members to the altar guild, inviting new members to shadow the more experienced members. The intent here is not only to convey knowledge but also to develop spiritual friendships and to knit that ministry community more tightly together. Another parish has invited new vestry members to partner with more senior members to learn about the ways in which the vestry works. This mentoring provides, again, the potential for deeper relationships within that small community. Older teenagers can be called on to welcome younger teenagers into youth ministries—the possibilities are varied and numerous. The larger point, however, is that for both the mentor and the one being mentored, the experience can provide a greater sense of ownership.

Ministry moments

Give ministries an opportunity to speak about their work in the services on Sunday and include prayers for that particular ministry in the Prayers of the People. Such a "ministry moment" helps communicate information about the many ministries in a community and builds on the notion that every member of the church is a minister. It challenges parishioners to talk about the ways that they see God at work in their midst. And if people speak publicly—during the worship service, no less—about the work that God is calling them to do, it deepens their sense of engagement with the ministry and sense of personal ownership over the church's ministry as a whole.

Financial stewardship

Money is by no means the only way that people can be invested in the community, but it is one of them. Churches create a sense of ownership by focusing on stewardship, recognizing the grace that has been given to us and responding to that grace by sharing it in terms of time, talent, and treasure. As people move along the spiritual continuum, giving patterns change. People move from paying "dues" to the church as one organization among many, keeping annual offerings the same, to thinking about proportional giving. And this need not be a focus just for a limited period in the fall months but an ongoing process, year-round.

Of course, there are many ways to develop this sense of ownership and investment in the spiritual life. But such ownership is not meant merely as an end in itself. It is meant as a way to strengthen the life of the congregation, so that the church can be of better service in the world. And that leads us to the last of the best practice principles: pastor the community.

Create Ownership

Questions
for Reflection

What are the pros and cons of speaking of ownership in relationship to a church?

Do you see creating ownership as a growth opportunity for your congregation?

Do members of your congregation ever view church as spectator sport? As entertainment?

What are ways to deepen a sense of participation in the life of the community?

6

Pastor the Community

William Temple, Archbishop of Canterbury in the 1940s, made this observation: the church is the only society that exists for the benefit of those who are not its members.

Whether that is exactly true could be argued, but the archbishop makes an important point about Christian community. Vital congregations are engaged with the entire community—not only the immediate community of church members but also with the neighborhood in which the church exists. And that vision of "neighborhood" can be as expansive as the global community. While many churches take on the air of a restricted social club, that is not the intention for the body of Christ.

The church is called to pastor the community, which suggests a healing, serving presence. This healing can only happen with an outward orientation, with engagement and understanding of what life in the community is like. Vital congregations pastor their community by listening for what is going on and seeking what God is already doing. It is not a matter of the church bringing God to the community. God is already present. Rather, pastoring the community recognizes that the church is an instrument in the healing work God intends for a broken world. Accordingly, it shouldn't be much of a surprise that this kind of connection with the world finds warrant throughout scripture.

❖ What Does Scripture Say About Pastoring the Community?

We return to the story of the children of Israel as they are about to enter the promised land. In five sermons found in the book of Deuteronomy, Moses instructs how they are to live in this new land and how they are to find and follow God's intention—and that includes consideration of the outsider. The passages speak for themselves:

> For the LORD your God is God of gods and Lord of lords, the great God, mighty and awesome, who is not partial and takes no bribe, who executes justice for the orphan and the widow, and who loves the strangers, providing them food and clothing. You shall also love the stranger, for you were strangers in the land of Egypt.
>
> —Deuteronomy 10:17-19

> "Cursed be anyone who deprives the alien, the orphan, and the widow of justice." All the people shall say, "Amen!"
>
> —Deuteronomy 27:19

In the book of Leviticus, a book often associated with rigorous, even oppressive, rule-keeping we read:

> The alien who resides with you shall be to you as the citizen among you; you shall love the alien as yourself, for you were aliens in the land of Egypt: I am the LORD your God.
>
> —Leviticus 19:34

Later, as we read about the people of Israel taken into exile, we hear the word of Jeremiah spoken to those who find themselves situated in a foreign land. The prophet calls on the people to respond to forced exile by seeking the best for the city in which they dwell, which is another way of describing pastoring the community. Hear the words of the prophet:

> But seek the welfare of the city where I have sent you into exile, and pray to the LORD on its behalf, for in its welfare you will find your welfare.
>
> —Jeremiah 29:7

As we move to the gospels, we find Jesus engaging with the world beyond the bounds of his own community. Truth be told, the whole message of incarnation is a matter of reaching out. During his lifetime, he ventures outside the boundaries of Israel. He engages in conversation with a Syro-Phoenician woman, and he is apparently persuaded by the encounter to broaden his own sense of mission (Mark 7:24-30). He frees a demoniac from destructive possession, someone who was an outsider, someone that people in decent society feared and shunned (Mark 5:1-20). He meets the Samaritan woman at the well, something no respectable Jewish man might have done at that time, engaging with her in a discussion about worship and life of the spirit (John 4:4-26). He makes the Good Samaritan, an outsider, the hero of one of his most famous parables (Luke 10:25-37).

When Jesus commissions his disciples in Luke 10, he sends them out two by two into all the towns and instructs them to accept the hospitality of those places. They are not sent to tell those townspeople how to be. Rather, they are sent to offer peace, to meet the people where they are, to learn from them, to receive from them. That's quite a different model of missionary enterprise than that of many Christians over the centuries.

Service is a consistent theme in Jesus's instruction, captured well in the Gospel of Mark when he says that the Son of Man comes not to be served but to serve (Mark 10:45). This comes right after the disciples get in a heated debate about which one of them is the greatest. Jesus gets wind of this discussion and speaks about the greatness that comes with service, a theme that Martin Luther King Jr. picked up in a sermon just a few weeks before his assassination. In the book, *A Knock at Midnight*, editor Clayborne Carson shares these words from one of King's sermons: "Everybody can be great, because everybody can serve. You don't have to have a college degree to serve. You don't have to know about Plato and Aristotle to serve. You don't have to know Einstein's theory of relativity to serve. You don't have to know the second theory of thermodynamics in physics to serve. You only need a heart full of grace, a soul generated by love."

In the Sermon on the Mount, right after the Beatitudes, a list of what blessedness looks like in our world, Jesus offers two images for the intended impact of the disciples on the world beyond the walls of the church (Matthew 5:13-16). He tells the disciples that they are to be salt and light. As a metaphor, salt conveys a cleansing, healing, preserving presence. It also simply makes things more interesting. In addition, the disciples are called to be light in the world—not so that everyone will think how wonderful and charitable and kind the disciples are but so that people will see what God is up to. Jesus says to his followers, his students:

> You are the light of the world. A city on a hill cannot be hidden... let your light shine before others, so that they may see your good works and give glory to your Father in heaven.
>
> —Matthew 5:14-16

In Matthew 25:31-46, the parable of the sheep and the goats, a passage many have identified as a parable of judgment, Jesus comes down hard on those who refuse to help the poor, feed the hungry, clothe the naked, visit the prisoner. In contrast, those who engage with people in need are rewarded. That is, when we address the needs of those most marginalized, we meet the needs of Jesus himself.

The early church picked up these themes, as the Acts of the Apostles describes a church that reaches out beyond traditional boundaries to include those who have been excluded. A Roman centurion, for instance, a representative of an oppressive empire, becomes part of the community (Acts 10). An Ethiopian eunuch, an outsider in many respects, is baptized (Acts 8). Saint Paul wanders around Athens and begins his ministry there by first finding out about the religious customs of that community, and it is only once he has accomplished that primary task that he shares news of the Jesus Movement and its relevance for that community (Acts 17). Whenever the Acts of the Apostles chronicles dramatic growth in the church, it also proclaims that the church grew because outsiders looked at the community and said, "See how they love one another!"

The ministry of Saint Paul, not often considered radical, was actually an amazing departure from tradition as it articulated a radical and expansive vision that the church has never fully realized. In his letter to the Galatians, he writes:

> For in Christ Jesus you are all children of God through faith. As many of you were baptized into Christ have clothed yourselves with Christ. There is no longer Jew or Greek, there is no longer slave or free, there is no longer male and female; for all of you are one in Christ Jesus.
>
> —Galatians 3:26-28

The same message is echoed in the letter to the Colossians:

> In that renewal there is no longer Greek and Jew, circumcised and uncircumcised, barbarian, Scythian, slave and free; but Christ is all and in all!
>
> —Colossians 3:11

The Letter of James adds an important voice to the canon of Scripture, noting that faith without works is dead (James 2:17, 26). Similarly, the first Epistle of John notes that one cannot say they love God if they are not responding to needs around them (1 John 3:17).

Throughout the Bible, then, we see a constant concern for the communities in which the authors, characters, and audience reside. We are called to serve and care for our neighbors. We must contemplate our connections with the places in which God has embedded our ministries.

❖ What Does Our Liturgy Suggest About Pastoring the Community?

As in previous chapters, when it comes to the tradition set forth in our liturgy, we begin with baptism (always an excellent place to start!). We note the promises that the whole congregation makes as part of the baptismal covenant. There are five promises, and, notably, three of them are outwardly directed.

Will you proclaim by word and example the good news of God in Christ?

In other words, will the life you lead in the world convey good news? Episcopalians sometimes resist the notion that we are each and all preachers, but this promise says that our words and actions are indeed a light to the world. This promise invokes Saint Francis's noted injunction that we are to preach the gospel at all times—and, if necessary, use words. But we should not shy away from using words as well, not to compel belief but simply to share what God has done in our lives. That is evangelism in the best sense of the word.

Will you seek and serve Christ in all persons, loving your neighbor as yourself?

There is a powerful affirmation implicit in this promise, which is to say that Christ is somehow present *in* all persons. It doesn't say all Episcopalians. It doesn't say all Christians. It certainly doesn't identify race or nationality. It simply says that Christ is present in all people. All people are, in some respect, anointed by God, which is the basis for the call to love one's neighbor as oneself. If we truly buy into this notion, as amazing as it seems, it will transform our vision of pastoring the community. It will not be a matter of our beneficence (which can easily devolve into pride) but rather a sense of honoring all persons. The Indian religious tradition may be better at this than many Christians, as the salutation *namaste* indicates that the light in me sees and honors the light in you.

Will you strive for justice and peace among all people, and respect the dignity of every human being?

Yet another powerful affirmation is implied here, with the claim that every human being bears dignity. The call to strive for justice and peace recognizes that this involves intention and maybe even some hard work. But the promise also says that such work is indeed the work of the baptized community, recognizing there will not be peace without justice. We'll talk more about advocacy later in this chapter, but this last promise signals that pastoring the community means making a difference in a world too often marked by indifference and injustice.

Since it is true that our praying shapes our believing, we look to the prayers in the baptismal service for insight into what it means to pastor the community. As we pray for the candidates for ordination, we ask that they will be taught to love others in the power of the Spirit and that they will be sent out to the world in witness to God's love. So, disciples (followers of Jesus) become apostles (those who are sent). That apostolic mission is another way of describing what it means to pastor the community.

As we consider the liturgy for Holy Eucharist, we note that it is sometimes referred to as the mass (in Latin, *missa*), which is related to *mission*. This sustaining sacrament, sometimes described as bread for the journey, is meant to give us strength and courage to go out and do God's work in the world, to love and serve with gladness and singleness of heart. Soon after the post-communion prayer comes the dismissal, arguably the lynchpin of the entire liturgy. To make this point, as we noted in the introduction, some churches have put signs over the exit door, or perhaps at the exit to the parking lot, which state: "The worship is over. The service begins."

Jesus came to serve, and he is explicit that his followers are meant to do the same as a reflection of grace. A relationship with him is deepened, therefore, through commitment to service in the church and the neighborhood. Jesus calls his disciples to go out into the world and proclaim the good news by word and example. Fulfilling that call requires knowing what God is up to in the neighborhood already, listening to voices encountered there and entering into dialogue with those of other faiths. It's about working for justice and peace wherever suffering appears.

❖ How Extroverted Is Your Church?

As is true of each one of these best practice principles, change will not come quickly. We're not talking about some quick-fix, magical programs. We're talking about thinking in new ways about what many churches are already doing. It's a discernment process, and it begins by looking at the character, the personality of the congregation.

In our work with congregations, as discussed earlier in this book, we've noted three archetypes that are particularly prominent among Episcopal churches: extroverted churches, troubled churches, and complacent churches, all of which are described in Chapter 2. Extroverted churches often engage in the task of pastoring the community; they are deeply devoted to outreach, to mission, to faith in action, to service in the community. Indeed, Episcopal churches are distinctively strong in such outreach. The question that needs to be asked, however, is how the church's engagement with this kind of service different from other nonprofits or other civic organizations (like the Rotary Club).

Don't get us wrong. Those nonprofits and civic organizations do amazing work, which we hope and pray will continue and expand. But the church is a different kind of community. Accordingly, its outreach to the community should draw on an understanding of its spiritual connection. Churches take on this kind of work not because the church is filled with nice people, or guilty people, or generous people. Churches engage in such mission as an expression of discipleship, as an outgrowth of their love for God and neighbor. In short, it's a Jesus thing.

Extroverted churches, already committed to such service, are called to find ways to anchor those current service efforts to the faith. Many of these ways count on the initiative of community leadership: preaching and teaching about that connection, for instance. It may mean referring to the baptismal covenant or incorporating prayer and sharing pertinent scripture passages before or immediately after such service projects. If a church already has a ministry like a soup kitchen or a mission trip or a construction project, leaders can integrate scripture and prayer in those gatherings. And in the spirit of creating a sense of ownership, different members of the service team can be invited to take the lead in offering those prayers and scripture readings.

A congregation grows spiritually when its members participate in response to the needs that surround them in the community. Furthermore, many who seek a faith community will select a church based on how that community responds to needs outside the church. This kind of spirit can prove to be a powerful invitation for newcomers and inquirers seeking to identify with the congregation.

❖ How Can Churches Elevate Expectations In Pastoring the Community?

Best practice churches make it clear early and often that they count on congregants to serve the needs of both the church and the community. Again, this is where the role of the leader is central. Clergy and other leaders set the tone and pace for this commitment because, as Steve Gallimore of Tennessee Valley Community Church insists, "Your people will care no more than you do; they will go no farther than you will. It's that simple." As churches focus on community outreach, church leaders must first figure out ways to incorporate service into their very busy routines. Leaders model this particular aspect of discipleship, and then they coach congregants to fit service into their busy secular schedules, inspiring their people to make it a priority in the midst of busy lives.

❖ What Is God Up To In the Neighborhood?

Pastoring the community often begins with exploration and curiosity, with discovering what is going on in the neighborhood. Too often our churches have no relationship to neighbors. And even when they do try to cultivate such relationships, they frequently operate based on a memory of what the neighborhood used to be like. After all, churches are historical institutions that remain in place while surrounded by social and demographic shifts. It is paramount, then, that churches wishing to pastor their communities acknowledge the current reality of their neighborhoods, rather than assume the neighborhoods of twenty, thirty, or even just ten years ago.

One church in an affluent suburb recognized that it had grown distant from its community and looked for simple, non-threatening ways to start building a bridge. The rector invited the local fire department to come to the church after a Sunday service. She offered a blessing for their work and an expression of gratitude from the congregation. Children (of all ages) loved seeing the fire engines up close, and it was a great way for the church to connect with these public servants.

Immediately after 9/11, on the Sunday following that tragedy, an evening service held in a Manhattan church ended with a candlelight procession to a local firehouse a block away. That particular firehouse had lost a dozen people. It was a spontaneous expression of solidarity, cementing a relationship that has continued with an annual 9/11 memorial service.

In communities where police still ride horses (there are a few of them), churches have often invited those members of the police force

Pastor the Community

to the blessing of the animals. But, of course, a neighborhood is much more than its public safety personnel—or any particular group. It is critical, then, that in pastoring the community, a church does not restrict itself to ministering only to a specific group—lest the church only further contribute to polarization and isolation. Public blessings of animals, then, can serve as opportunities for reconciliation and community building, with police horses being blessed alongside service dogs and family pets. A broad invitation to a liturgy like the blessing of animals is one with wide appeal to a community. Who doesn't want to celebrate their beloved dog or cat with others?

After discussing ideas for outreach with neighboring churches in the diocese, a church in Hawaii implemented a "bread walk," where members would walk around the church's neighborhood, delivering loaves of freshly baked bread. Up to that point, they had not been particularly engaged with the neighborhood, and very few parishioners lived in the blocks surrounding the church. One participant described the event:

> The loaves were baked and ready to go, and we went off in twos and threes. We knocked on doors, some of which were opened, some of which were not. We met so many people, most of whom knew nothing about our church beyond its location. We shared bread and explained that we simply wanted to introduce ourselves to the community and to share something with our neighbors. We asked how we could be a good neighbor. If they were interested, we told them a bit about some of the things we do.

Responses to the bread walk were different than expected. One homeowner invited parishioners into her yard so the kids could climb a treehouse and play on the swing set. Another homeowner was an avid gardener who shared plants for church members to take home. Others shared their own stories of the neighborhood, which gave parishioners a much better sense of the relational dynamics in the community—something that they never would have known otherwise. The participant reflected on the impact of the bread walk:

I think, to some degree, I went into the bread walk thinking about how it could help us grow our church, to encourage more people to consider it as a possible spiritual home for themselves. I came out of it full of gratitude that we were graced with these visits with our church neighbors, their stories, and their joy in receiving.... I don't know exactly how many people we met attended a service or event at our church after that, and to be honest, that is not what really mattered. The truly wonderful thing that happened was the connections we made with people.

Consider another approach to engagement with the neighborhood, this process designed by Woodley, the canon for ministry support in the Diocese of Long Island. She notes that one of the key characteristics of many congregations is that they are not in significant contact with their surrounding communities. Many of these congregations reflect on their positive experiences with family and church in years past. Often, they are locked firmly in that past, focused on what worked well then. But they have lost touch with their neighbors today. To help congregations move out of that past and into a present-day engagement, she encourages congregational leaders to convene a community panel (either live or online).

The community panel is made up of people in service to the community: the town planner, local social service agencies, hospital, police department, local school leadership, and community faith leaders. The panel members are informed that the parish is seeking vision forward in a changing world. They are each given ten minutes to share their responses to three questions:

1. How do you see your work and who do you serve?

2. What are the greatest challenges and opportunities that you see on the horizon for the people you serve?

3. Where do you see hope and what are you building on?

Woodley has found that the community panel completely changes a church's understanding of its particular call to ministry, with ramifications throughout its program planning. Information that comes forward reconnects the congregation in vital ways to their community. Visions of partnerships and mission alignment emerge. Pathways of vision, understanding, clarity and agility become apparent. Woodley says that giving the Holy Spirit the opportunity to speak from other sources is inspiring and uplifting for everyone involved, the community as well as the congregation.

Church to go

In recent years, Ash Wednesday observance has included "Ashes to Go" at many churches in America and around the world. While she was not the originator, Emily Mellott was a key player in facilitating widespread practice of this offering. It began as she decided to offer ashes at the commuter train station a block away from her house, since many people who came to her early Ash Wednesday service were on their way to work. The offering was very well-received, and Mellott heard of a couple other churches doing a similar thing. She presented the idea at a diocesan convention in Chicago, and soon, clergy across the country were offering Ashes to Go. Mellott writes:

> Three moments stick with me from that first Ash Wednesday at the train station: a pair of commuters hanging over the station rail, above where we were, taking photos on their phones and marveling out loud at what seemed extraordinary—the church coming out on the sidewalk in the cold; a man who went home and brought his infant granddaughter back to one of our lay volunteers because he just wanted her to be prayed for; a young man who told us that it was his second day sober and who wasn't sure what came next—but he and we recognized the deep connection of the symbol of repentance, and the Ash Wednesday prayer that God make new hearts within us, to where he was, that particular raw morning. (*You can find a longer report on the experience in the appendix*).

This kind of effort of bringing the church to the people, of taking the church outside the walls, need not only happen on Ash Wednesday.

Episcopal priest Adrian Dannhauser has written a soon-to-be published book entitled *Ask Me For A Blessing*, in which she talks about how she brings blessing to the sidewalks of New York:

> My church sits on Madison Avenue at 35th Street in New York City, one block from the Empire State Building. There are loads of passersby all day long. The vast majority of them don't venture inside the church, of course. But the constant foot traffic creates the perfect setup for an Episcopal priest with a penchant for chatting up strangers with an encouraging word.
>
> One morning a week, I stand on the sidewalk right outside the church doors. I put on my vestments and put out a chalkboard A-frame sign. It's the kind of sign that restaurants, bars, and coffee shops use to list the day's specials or display catchy phrases like "Rosé All Day" and "Congratulations! You made it out of bed." My catchy phrase is this: "Ask me for a blessing. God's grace is meant to be shared." I write it in on the board, wipe the chalk dust from my hands, and then just kind of stand there. I try to look open and friendly but not overly eager or desperate. It's an art, really.
>
> Over the next thirty minutes, most people will walk by me without making eye contact. Several will smile and nod or say good morning. Ten or so might actually stop and take me up on the offer of a blessing. All things considered, that's a pretty decent turnout. I suppose it doesn't hurt that New Yorkers tend to be bolder than most, as evidenced by the many questions I get. "Are you a nun?" is the most common. "Can I take your picture?" is a close second.
>
> It's no surprise that many people don't know what to make of me and my "blessing booth," of sorts. I realize that the whole thing is weird to begin with, but especially for those who have little to no religious frame of reference.

Dinner conversation: God in my life...

One parishioner who was quite involved in her church wondered about how to engage coworkers at her law firm. They were hard-working, highly ethical, kind people who seemed to have no religious observance. She decided she would have a dinner party, inviting a dozen people. And she would tell them that the dinner conversation would be a matter of completing the sentence: God in my life....

She felt she needed clergy backup, so she asked a priest to join the dinner, though both priest and host were not sure how the evening would go. Would anyone show up? Would anyone have anything to say? Would it get contentious? After initial chitchat over drinks, the guests sat to dinner, and discussion began. Every person had a story to tell. And there seemed to be little reticence about sharing. It was clear to both host and priest that people do indeed have a hunger to explore a life with God. These days, that may not readily happen in the institutional church, but the hunger remains. Creative minds and hospitable spirits will help figure out ways to explore that hunger.

Uniting local clergy

Many of our churches operate in silos, never interacting with other faith communities in their towns or even in their dioceses or denominations. Often congregations compete with each other instead of offering mutual support. But it doesn't have to be that way. Vital congregations establish strong relationships (and even partnerships) with other churches, nonprofits, and community leaders. They do this for two reasons: to remain involved with the most pressing community needs and to generate the greatest possible impact by working shoulder-to-shoulder with others to address those needs.

The rector or senior pastor can take the lead in working with other local clergy to identify issues of concern to the community, which will naturally change over time. These issues and concerns will vary from community to community. In one community, a string of teenage suicides brought the clergy together for prayer and coordinated response. The clergy hosted an open forum for the community, offering pastoral resources and education, as well as a ministry of presence in a difficult, anxiety producing time. While church attendance in this town had dwindled in all of the denominations, this forum was standing room only. Other communities work to address issues of substance abuse among youth. Needs for hunger and shelter persist in many places. Many of these issues are simply too big for just one congregation to address.

Vital congregations can participate in local community groups that address issues like education, healthcare, affordable housing, issues reflected in the baptismal covenant that call us to work for justice and peace. This kind of activity draws lay leaders into collaboration with other congregations' lay leaders and exposes the congregation to community needs about which they might not have been informed. It also identifies the congregation as a place that cares about the needs of the community, a great way to welcome newcomers to your faith community.

❖ What Are Some Other Opportunities For Growth In Pastoring the Community?

Interfaith dialogue

A persistent question among contemporary Christians is how we relate to other faiths. One way to pastor the local community is to develop partnerships and conversations of both an ecumenical and interfaith nature. Leadership can suggest readings and can facilitate discussion, in the confidence that encounter with the "other" provides a way to gain deeper clarity about what one's own community believes.

One small church that didn't have full-time clergy came to a new vision of who were their neighbors. They invited members of a mosque located within a mile of their church to join for several gatherings. There had been no such outreach before. They held a tea for the ladies of the mosque and their own parish. They shared meals together at the mosque and at their church with men and women. Parents and children had play dates on the parish playground. The church opened their play area to the children in the neighborhood. All kinds of relationships were formed where they had not previously existed.

Direct encounter

Some churches see their outreach as primarily a matter of making grants, and sharing financial resources. That's obviously commendable. It can be transformative for ministries that are financially strapped. At the same time, pastoring the community suggests an intentional push to balance grant-making from the operating budget and fundraising sources with hands-on opportunities for parishioners to be of service. Our research confirms that spiritual growth is ultimately relational. While writing a check is certainly important, it is no substitute for direct encounter with those in need. As Jesus says, the harvest is plentiful. There is no congregation in our nation that does not live in proximity to both spiritual and physical need. As mentioned earlier, vital congregations challenge every member to be involved in some aspect of service, since service is one of the key indicators of that vitality.

Back-to-school partnerships

Many churches explore the possibility of partnership with a local public school to provide support for teachers and students. Schools are natural community centers. Tutoring and other hands-on service are powerful ways to pastor the community, especially its children. A great byproduct emerges when members of the same faith community work together in support of young people, their families, and teachers in this way.

Globalizing the neighborhood

The times in which we live call us to envision our community as global. As our baptismal covenant calls us to seek and serve Christ in all persons, to respect the dignity of every human being, we are called to recognize our connection with all God's children, our global responsibility. The character of the Anglican Communion helps connect us in that way. Many kinds of partnerships are accessible to Episcopal congregations and dioceses, thanks to this worldwide network. We have an array of resources available through organizations like Episcopal Relief & Development that provide ways to pastor and partner with communities on other continents.

As part of a broader vision of pastoring the community, the role of advocacy becomes important. It offers an important way to strive for justice and peace. Christians can be "salt and light" in the world by making their voices heard among political and economic leaders. These voices gain impact when many come together around an issue. Many denominations, including the Episcopal Church, have offices dedicated to this kind of work, offering education on particular issues as well as bringing in different voices and perspectives to bear on those issues. Other organizations like Sojourners can bring a Christian perspective to the work for justice and peace. Advocacy becomes one more way of providing service.

As churches build relationships with government agencies, opportunities may arise for financial resources to be made in the form of grants to church outreach efforts. Jesus told his disciples to be as wise as serpents and as harmless as doves. Part of that wisdom piece is to recognize that, in certain circumstances, there are government and foundation funds available for doing things like feeding the poor and providing housing for the homeless.

❖ What Lessons Might the Church Learn From the Past?

As we consider how the church pastors the community, it's clear the church has a history with which it must reckon. With that in mind, perhaps one of the most important ways churches can pastor the wider community these days is to admit where the church has gotten it wrong and when it has actively participated or been complicit in injustices over the centuries.

A model for this work is the Truth and Reconciliation Commission that unfolded in the wake of South African apartheid. While Archbishop Desmond Tutu famously noted that there was no future without forgiveness, he also taught that we can't get there too quickly. We can't get there without admitting ways that we and our ancestors have fallen short, the ways that people of privilege currently benefit from past injustices. For the church in the United States, and perhaps especially for the Episcopal Church, this includes telling the truth about how the church aligned itself with empire, and how Indigenous Americans, African Americans, and Latino/Hispanic and Asian communities have been treated. We commend the Sacred Ground curriculum, provided by the office of the Presiding Bishop, as we helpful and healing way to explore our history.

Biblical resources of lament and repentance are vital. There are many ways congregations may explore their own histories and seek reconciliation. Remember the baptismal covenant, the second promise of which asks whether we will persevere in resisting evil and, whenever we fall into sin, repent, and return to the Lord. Perhaps, then, for many churches, we cannot effectively pastor the community until we have come to terms with the ways that we have fallen into sin ourselves and are called to repentance.

A big reason churches should be involved in pastoring the community is that churches learn in the process. As Jesus says, when we give, we receive. Churches may discover when they have been wrong or where they have thought too narrowly. As churches engage with others in the community—especially those who are not involved in church, or who may have left church for any number of reasons—the church then comes to deeper understanding of its mission. This all is captured in a beautiful collect for the church, found in the Book of Common Prayer on p. 816:

> Gracious Father, we pray for thy holy Catholic Church. Fill it with all truth, in all truth with all peace. Where it is corrupt, purify it; where it is in error, direct it; where in any thing it is amiss, reform it. Where it is right, strengthen it; where it is in want, provide for it; where it is divided, reunite it; for the sake of Jesus Christ thy Son our Savior. *Amen.*

Merging service and evangelism

Evangelism is a topic that doesn't always sit well with Episcopalians, often for good reason. The history of the church has been marked by people who confused sharing good news with compelling doctrinal agreement. As columnist Dave Barry observes: "People who want to share their religious views with you almost never want you to share yours with them."

At the same time, a reluctance toward evangelism may come from a sense of complacency or perhaps even an elitist vision of the church as a social club that only welcomes certain classes of people. That's been a historical challenge for the Episcopal Church in the United States. We've recalled earlier in this book how one woman commented to her rector: "I don't know why you all are talking about welcoming new people. Everyone who ought to be an Episcopalian in town already is."

But as we see in the baptismal covenant, we promise to proclaim by word and example the good news of God in Christ. In other words, sharing good news in word and deed is not an option, even if we need to work through some convoluted history about how we feel about evangelism. Leaders seeking to apply best practice principles see a natural affinity between sharing the gospel and serving those who are struggling and broken. Those who feel hopeless have hearts that are fertile ground for a message of grace. As the Letter of James says, "Faith without works is dead." There's a synergy between the ways we express our faith and the ways we live our lives. Both are necessary. If we can combine evangelism with service, then, we can demonstrate that helping others is not just a platform for the gospel, but it is the gospel.

As we conclude our review of these five best practice principles, we see that they are interconnected. Service that comes with *pastoring the community* can be a powerful way to *get people moving* along the spiritual journey, *creating ownership* of ministries among congregants, *embedding scripture* throughout such work. And none of it can happen without an engaged *heart of the leader.*

Questions
for Reflection

In what ways does your congregation pastor the community?
Do you know what God is up to in your neighborhood?

What is the connection between Sunday worship and service
in the community?

How is service in your community different from the good work
of other nonprofits?

How do you see spiritual growth enhanced by service and
outreach?

Conclusion

Where Do We Go from Here?

The challenge to the church, and to the culture, is significant, and there continues to be a great deal of conversation about what comes next. Of course, this is not the first time people of faith have had this conversation. Throughout this book, we have considered the scriptural warrant for the work that we believe churches are called to do. In the stories of the Bible, we find again and again that people have had to wonder: What comes next?

In the Old Testament, the children of Israel wander for years in a circuitous route in the wilderness until they arrive at the shores of the Jordan. There, they consider what life in the promised land will look like as they are about to step into a future that God had prepared. Later in exile, those same people seek a way home, without knowing when or how that might come. Regardless of the uncertainty, they hold on to the promise of home.

In the New Testament, Jesus gathers a group of disciples, forming the Jesus Movement with the simple invitation: Follow me. There is no job description. No strategic plan. No disclosed destination. Simply an invitation to a journey built on trust in a relationship with him. At the conclusion of the gospel narrative, as the disciples watch the resurrected Christ ascend into heaven, one can imagine them looking at each other and saying: Now what? What's next? Of course, they soon experience the power of the Spirit in Pentecost, which leads them out to change the world in ways that none of them could have expected. They turn the world upside down.

Throughout the scriptures, we find a persistent theme that new life emerges from a seed that has fallen into the ground and seems to be dead. But dead ends suddenly become thresholds. This is more about resurrection than it is about resuscitation. It is in God's character to make all things new, a truth revealed in the first pages of Genesis. God looks at the handiwork of the first six days and declares it to be very good. That same truth is promised in the closing chapters of the book of Revelation as God holds out the promise of a new heaven and a new earth. In each of these passages, God invites us to join in the process of creation, to participate in this new work.

As we embrace this theme for the church today, confident that God will act as God has acted in the past, we remain hopeful there is a new chapter for our congregations.

We commend to your consideration these five best practice principles. We encourage you to see how they might apply to your context. Try those you suspect will be useful and prayerfully and honestly reflect upon both your successes and failures. Some principles may already be at work in your congregation. You may think of ways to expand and build upon these principles. You may realize that your congregation has not considered one or more of these principles. You may sense great growth opportunities in front of you.

We hope that identifying these best practice principles and sharing such a variety of practices from vital congregations can offer a way forward, paving the way for spiritual growth and a deeper love of God and neighbor. Perhaps this book may even jump start a congregation whose battery seems dead. We believe renewal can come to any context.

Perhaps the most important thing we can do, however, is pray, an expression of confidence in the one who is called the God of the living and not of the dead.

We conclude this discussion as we began, with a prayer from the Book of Common Prayer, one found in the services for ordination of a bishop and a priest as well as in the services for Good Friday and the Great Vigil of Easter. It recognizes that any signs of life in the church come at the gracious hand of God, the one who graciously gives life:

> O God of unchangeable power and eternal light: Look favorably on your whole Church, that wonderful and sacred mystery; by the effectual working of your providence, carry out in tranquility the plan of salvation; let the whole world see and know that things which were being cast down are being raised up, and things which had grown old are being made new, and that all things are being brought to their perfection by him through whom all things were made, your Son Jesus Christ our Lord; who lives and reigns with you, in the unity of the Holy Spirit, one God, for ever and ever. *Amen.*

If you do nothing else in your congregations, pray this prayer. May God richly bless you and your communities as you seek to grow.

Questions
for Reflection

Based on what you have read, what one or two things would you like for your congregation to work on?

Where do you see a need for culture change in your congregation?

Do you believe God can bring renewed life to your congregation? To your own spiritual life?

Appendix

Introduction

RenewalWorks: Learn more at RenewalWorks.org.

Footsteps: Making Spiritual Growth the Priority by Jay Sidebotham. Available at ForwardMovement.org.

Chapter 1: Archetypes of the Spiritual Journey

When "Fine" Isn't Enough
Written by Brenda Husson and Ryan Fleenor and originally published in March 2019 on ECF Vital Practices. Used with permission.

Everything was fine. Certainly that's how St. James' parishioners felt and the way other parishes and clergy viewed us. We had four services on Sunday, a thriving Sunday school and the parents that come with it, twenty- and thirty-year olds as well as older adults. Forums on Sunday were well attended, and we were feeding and sheltering some of our low-income and homeless neighbors as well as sending volunteers to Malawi and Haiti and working with the children of incarcerated parents here in New York City. Our programmatic life was humming along.

However, whenever parishioners were asked what they loved about St. James', they always spoke first about the sense of community they found here. It's hard to complain about that (and it is a great community), but there was no talk of transformation or God, let alone Jesus. And stewardship (again, fine by the standards of many parishes) was flat, indicating that we were, for many of our parishioners, just another nonprofit—maybe their favorite but not a place that was changing or challenging them at the center of their lives.

I was flummoxed. And, as the rector, discouraged. Yet I hardly felt there was much reason to complain when everything was "fine." Fortunately, a trusted friend and mentor, the Rev. Carol Anderson, was willing to listen to me whine. But only briefly. Then she pointed out that unless I was willing to change everything so that we were focused only on creating disciples—parishioners who wanted to follow Jesus and take up the call to love God with their whole heart and mind and strength and their neighbor as themselves—I shouldn't expect much to shift.

Some serious soul-searching and conversation ensued. We had conversations with staff, both clergy and lay, and with the vestry. It turned out that despite the overwhelming sense that everything was going well, once the possibility of "more" was raised, excitement (and anxiety) grew. It helped that the "more" was not about doing more but rather a sense that church and our life of faith could mean more for all of us if we could find ways to grow spiritually. It also helped to acknowledge that this might mean stopping some of what we were doing if it wasn't leading people deeper into discipleship. As we laid out the idea of focusing all that we did during the week as well as on Sunday on knowing and following Christ, a lay staff member started to tear up. "Really? We could do that?" she said. "That's why I wanted to work in a church." Her comment was a gift but also a tough lesson. She had not known that until that moment.

As we began to reimagine our parish life, we learned about RenewalWorks, a ministry of Forward Movement. Using data drawn from more than 1,000 parishes across multiple denominations, they have shown that in spiritually vital congregations, parishioners are developing spiritual practices and disciplines. RenewalWorks provides no set program to fix what ails parishes, but they know from the research that the key indices for spiritual vitality are:

> reading and reflecting on scripture
>
> embracing core Christian beliefs
>
> engaging in personal spiritual practices
>
> serving those in need
>
> and being in a spiritual community.

All of that moves people along a continuum, from exploring faith to growing in faith to deepening faith in Christ and finally, to being centered in Christ. The RenewalWorks process provides a wonderful diagnostic tool—the spiritual vitality survey—to help congregations discover where parishioners are and what they need to move forward.

A high percentage of our parishioners completed the survey (a blizzard that kept everyone home for two days helped). The results were clarifying—and distressing. The clear majority of our parishioners were in the first two stages of spiritual growth (exploring and growing) with many reporting no real sense of core Christian beliefs or how to pray. Despite our efforts at engaging people with the Bible, it still felt like a foreign country to many. It was cold comfort to know we were well within the norm for Episcopal parishes. But it was also galvanizing.

The results underscored the fact that no matter how compelling worship is, unless everything points towards Christ and the path of discipleship, that weekly hour won't be enough to change people. Fortunately, RenewalWorks asks congregations to form a task force and helps process the results of the survey so that the task force can formulate plans to go forward, plans developed from the expressed needs and longings of the congregation.

Here's a sample of how St. James' moved forward: The rows of chairs facing the 'teacher' in Sunday forums changed to round tables where parishioners spoke with each other with some prompts and questions from a facilitator. From trying out prayer practices (we also had retreats where parishioners could learn ways to pray) to Bible study to conversations about Faith's Big Questions, the forum room has become electric with conversation and insight. We launched a catechumenate, using Forward Movement's free curriculum, *Transforming Questions,* and have a dozen people each year who commit ten weeks to exploring the fundamentals of the faith. There are Bibles in the pews, and they are used during sermons. Education for Ministry (EfM) has blossomed. Parishioners now lead morning and evening prayer five days a week. Two hundred parishioners, from 18 months to 95 years old, went on a Parish Weekend Away to explore the Book of Ruth! Small groups, formerly a struggle to launch and sustain, took off with 70 people committed to spending a season exploring the Apostles Creed. The list goes on.

When we retook the survey three years later, we learned that the congregation had changed. Now, the majority of our parishioners are in the second and third stages of spiritual growth. But here's one of the bests indices of a changed parish. After we had explained the first survey results to the parish and inaugurated the RenewalWorks process, a parishioner had asked, tongue only partially in cheek, "Does this mean we can talk about Jesus in the halls now?"

"Yes," we said then. And now we do.

Chapter 2: The Heart of the Leader

Learn more about *Revive*, a small-group discipleship program to equip lay leaders to be spiritual leaders: ForwardMovement.org.

A letter from Evelyn Underhill to Archbishop of Canterbury Cosmo Gordon Lang (Found among her papers, c.1930, and available at anglicanlibrary.org).

MAY it please your Grace: I desire very humbly to suggest with bishops assembled at Lambeth that the greatest and most necessary work they could do at the present time for the spiritual renewal of the Anglican Church would be to call the clergy as a whole, solemnly and insistently to a greater interiority and cultivation of the personal life of prayer. This was the original aim of the founders of the Jerusalem Chamber Fellowship, of whom I am one. We were convinced that the real failures, difficulties and weaknesses of the Church are spiritual and can only be remedied by spiritual effort and sacrifice, and that her deepest need is a renewal, first in the clergy and through them in the laity; of the great Christian tradition of the inner life. The Church wants not more consecrated philanthropists, but a disciplined priesthood of theocentric souls who shall be tools and channels of the Spirit of God: and this she cannot have until Communion with God is recognized as the first duty of the priest. But under modern conditions this is so difficult that unless our fathers in God solemnly require it of us, the necessary efforts and readjustments will not be made. With the development of that which is now called "The Way of Renewal" more and more emphasis has been placed on the nurture and improvement of the intellect, less and less, on that of the soul. I do not underrate the importance of the intellectual side of religion. But all who do personal religious work know that the real hunger among the laity is not for halting attempts to reconcile theology and physical science, but for the deep things of the Spirit.

We look to the Church to give us an experience of God, mystery, holiness, and prayer which, though it may not solve the antinomies of the natural world, shall lift us to contact with the supernatural world and minister eternal life. We look to the clergy to help and direct our spiritual growth. We are seldom satisfied because with a few noble exceptions they are so lacking in spiritual realism, so ignorant of the laws and experiences of the life of prayer. Their Christianity as a whole is humanitarian rather than theocentric. So their dealings with souls are often vague and amateurish. Those needing spiritual help may find much kindliness, but seldom that firm touch of firsthand knowledge of interior ways which comes only from a disciplined personal life of prayer. In public worship they often fail to evoke the spirit of adoration because they do not possess it themselves. Hence the dreary character of many church services and the result in the increasing alienation of the laity from institutional forms.

God is the interesting thing about religion, and people are hungry for God. But only a priest whose life is soaked in prayer, sacrifice, and love can, by his own spirit of adoring worship, help us to apprehend Him. We ask the bishops... to declare to the Church and especially its ministers, that the future of organized Christianity hinges not on the triumph of this or that type of churchman's theology or doctrine, but on the interior spirit of poverty, chastity, and obedience of the ordained. However difficult and apparently unrewarding, care for the interior spirit is the first duty of every priest. Divine renewal can only come through those whose roots are in the world of prayer.

THE TWO things that the laity want from the priesthood are spiritual realism and genuine love of souls. It is by these that all Christian successes have been won in the past and it is to these that men always respond. We instantly recognize those services and sermons that are the outward expression of the priest's interior adherence to God and the selfless love of souls. These always give us a religious experience. On the other hand, every perfunctory service, every cold and slovenly celebration (for these are more frequent than the bishops realize because when they are present, everything is at its best), is a lost opportunity which discredits corporate worship and again reflects back to the poor and shallow quality of the Priest's inner life... It is perhaps worthwhile to recall the humbling fact that recent notable secessions to the Roman Catholic communion have been caused by declaration by a felt need of the supernatural which the Church of England failed to satisfy, while the astonishing success of the Oxford Group Movement among young people of the educated class witnesses to the widespread desire for an experience of God unmet by the ordinary ministrations of the Church. History shows that these quasi-mystical movements among the laity do not flourish where the invisible side of institutional religion is vigorously maintained.

I know that recovering the ordered interior life of prayer and meditation will be very difficult for clergy immersed increasingly in routine work. It will mean for many a complete rearrangement of values and a reduction of social activities. They will not do it unless they are made to feel its crucial importance. This will not be achieved through "schools of prayer" which stimulate the mind rather than the spirit. But the solemn voice of the united episcopate, recalling the Church to that personal, realistic contact with the Supernatural which has been since Pentecost the one source of her power, will give authoritative support to those who already feel the need of a deeper spirituality and will remind the others that the renewal of a spiritual society must depend on giving absolute priority to the spiritual life.

I venture to put before the conference the following practical recommendations: (1) Education of Ordinands—That the bishops shall emphasize the need and importance of a far more thorough, varied, interesting and expert devotional training in our theological colleges which, with a few striking exceptions, seem to me to give insufficient attention to this vital part of their work. (2) The Clergy—That they should call upon every ordained clergyman, as an essential part of his pastoral duty and not merely for his own sake: (a) To adopt a rule of life which shall include a fixed daily period of prayer and reading of a type that feeds, pacifies and expands his soul, and deepens his communion with God; b) To make an annual retreat; (c) To use every endeavour to make his church into a real home of prayer and teach his people, both by exhortation and example so to use it.

Profiles from the Diocese of Washington:
Qualities We Seek in a Priest

Our ordained leaders collectively will be multicultural and racially diverse, to reflect the breadth of humanity represented in our mission area. They will be mission-focused, entrepreneurial, collaborative, and adaptive. The qualities described here are not exhaustive—nor are these qualities exclusive to priestly ministry. They are the result of much discernment and many conversations amidst clergy, lay leaders, congregations, and other dioceses. We do not expect every candidate for the priesthood to exhibit all of these qualities, but we do expect them to exhibit most of them. Our discernment process will focus on discerning the presence, or the seeds of presence, of these qualities and abilities in each candidate.

1) Compelling spiritual life and a passion for the Gospel: There is great spiritual hunger in the culture at large and in our congregations. The Diocese seeks clergy who love God with heart, mind, and soul, and who know Christ and seek to make Christ known. Our clergy will have a vision for the Episcopal Church's ministry and how to guide our people to greater faithfulness and spiritual depth. They will have both a deep reverence for the sacraments at the heart of our liturgical life and a sacramental worldview in which outward and visible things reveal inward and invisible truths.

2) Ability to communicate the Gospel in ways that people and communities find engaging and relevant to their lives: Communication is multi-faceted. Today's clergy need to speak several "languages," both human and technological, from the pulpit, in personal conversation and in social media. They are called to minister in a wide variety of contexts, among all sorts of people. There is a particular, urgent need to reach younger generations—families raising children, teenagers and young adults—as well as the ability to be an effective spiritual presence among our fastest growing demographic, those over the age of 75.

3) Spiritual maturity, self-awareness, and authenticity: The work of the Episcopal priesthood is challenging. It requires a strong spiritual center, physical and mental stamina, healthy personal boundaries, and a willingness to grow and learn alongside others. Effective clergy must be able to persevere in challenging circumstances, recognize their personal growth edges, and be willing to learn new skills and ask for help.

4) Ability to lead, organize, and equip others in ministry: Many people are drawn to the priesthood for the love of ministry—pastoral care, teaching, service, and speaking out for justice. The predominant model of ministry in most Episcopal churches is that of one minister

(the priest) ministering to all the people, or at the center of the Church's ministry. We seek a new paradigm, of clergy able to equip others for meaningful Christian lives and vocations, inviting others into the life of Christian community and ministry. It will require community organizing skills and the ability to identify and mentor new leaders.

5) Entrepreneurial leadership: We seek individuals who are able to take risks and try new things in ministry. Twenty-first century clergy need creativity, the capacity to discern new paths, and the willingness to make mistakes and learn from them. Entrepreneurial leaders see opportunities where others see decline; possibilities where others see insurmountable challenges.

6) The ability to lead congregations through change: The majority of our congregations face significant adaptive challenges. This generation of clergy will lead our congregations through the wilderness of life as it has been to the Promised Land to which God calls us. As with our spiritual ancestors, there is a process of transformation required of us on the journey, as well as the ability to adapt to new ways of being the Church. Our clergy will lead the way, in faithfulness to God's call and in the challenging work of change.

7) A willingness and ability to be vocationally flexible: Our churches are in a variety of contexts in a variety of locations with a variety of needs. Our clergy will need to respond to this variety with their own flexibility. Few are likely to serve in one role at one type of church in one city for their entire vocation. In addition, a growing number of congregations require clergy leaders that do not depend on them for their entire livelihood. Thus, we need some priests who can offer their presence and their gifts as priests in a part-time or non-stipendiary capacity. Our clergy will demonstrate flexibility in their vision of professional ministry in order to respond to God's call to them and the church in our world.

Source: edow.org/wp-content/uploads/sites/2/2021/10/Discernment_Manual.pdf

Vital signs of healthy parishes

Compelling Mission & Vision. A healthy parish has a clear understanding of its mission, states the mission clearly, and creates ministries which align to that mission. The mission is shared and supported by all levels of ministry leadership, lay and ordained.

Clear Path of Discipleship. A healthy parish has a path of discipleship for members of all ages and stages of life. This discipleship path is clearly articulated, has multiple on-ramps, and provides growth opportunities for all to engage in formation and ministries.

Faithful Financial Practices. A healthy parish utilizes financial best practices such as transparency, on-time reporting to the diocese, and forecasting sustainable budgeting. Finances are a faithful conversation, understood as Christian stewardship and formation.

Inspiring & Capable Leadership. A healthy parish invests in continuing education, training, and rest for its lay and ordained leaders, who are nurtured, valued and appreciated.

Welcoming & Connecting Ministries. A healthy parish is intentional and strategic about welcoming guests; it is prepared to invite and provide next step connections. Guests are valued. Welcoming ministries are dependent on the leadership of active lay members.

Uplifting & Inviting Worship. A healthy parish gathers for worship that engages people with inspirational experiences and relevant teaching; it engages and offers full participation to all. While shaped by our Episcopal ethos, worship expresses the cultural and ethnic heritage of members and the surrounding community.

Blessing Our Community. A healthy parish advocates for and partners with the local community and other organizations. This engagement focuses on the welfare of our neighbors and justice initiatives such as food scarcity, racial inequities, and immigration concerns. The parish is invested in the health and well-being of its local community.

Source: edow.org/wp-content/uploads/sites/2/2021/10/Vital_Signs_of_Parish_Health-2.pdf

Episcopal Church Foundation offers some examples of vestry covenants on their website at ecfvp.org/vestry-papers/article/662/vestry-covenants. Another resource is the *Vestry Resource Guide*, available in English and Spanish, availabe at Forward Movement at ForwardMovement.org

Chapter 3: Get People Moving

Invite Welcome Connect: Learn more at InviteWelcomeConnect. org or the book, *Invite Welcome Connect: Stories & Tools to Transform Your Church* by Mary Parmer available at Forward Movement at ForwardMovement.org

My Way of Love: Learn more at episcopalchurch.org/way-of-love/my-way-of-love

Christian Essentials from Christ Church Charlotte: Learn more at christchurchcharlotte.org/christian-essentials/

Life-line exercise: A poster of the life-line exercise (and other materials) can be found at RenewalWorks.org/resources/

Chapter 4: Embed Scripture in Everything

Ways to read the Bible as a congregation

- *The Path,* published by Forward Movement
- *The Bible Challenge:* Visit thecenterforbiblicalstudies.org
  Books available through Forward Movement
- *The Story,* published by Zondervan

Daily Devotionals

- *Forward Day by Day*: Available in print, online, as an app, and as a podcast. Also available in English, Spanish, Braille, and Large Print. ForwardMovement.org
- The Good Book Club: Learn more at GoodBookClub.org

Chapter 5: Create Ownership

The Way of Love: Learn more at episcopalchurch.org/way-of-love

Sample of parish prayer for renewal

Saint John's Episcopal Church, Memphis, Tennessee

> Come Holy Spirit, Fill the hearts of your faithful and kindle in them the fire of your love. Send for your spirit and they shall be created. And you shall renew the face of the earth. O, God, who by the light of the Holy Spirit, did instruct the hearts of the faithful, grant that by the same Holy Spirit we may be truly wise and ever enjoy His consolations. *Amen.*

Listening Hearts: Discerning Call in Community by Suzanne G. Farnham, Joseph P. Gill, R. Taylor McLean, and Susan M. War: Available at listeninghearts.org.

Spiritual gifts inventory prepared by the ELCA (Evangelical Lutheran Church in America) and edited for an Episcopal audience by Claire Woodley: spiritualgiftquiz.org.

Chapter 6: Pastor the Community

Ashes to Go
by Emily Mellott, Used with permission

Ashes to Go and its variants started independently in several locations. I first got involved when it occurred to me that since many of the folks who came to our early Ash Wednesday service were trying to get ashes on their way to work, we might serve both our congregation and the community better by offering ashes at the commuter train station just a block away. I was inspired by the example of a friend who was part of an ecumenical group who had offered ashes at a neighborhood coffee shop for several years before.

I had a strong sense that I didn't know what we were doing, but I recruited a few volunteers from my congregation, printed a little leaflet with some appropriate prayers, and we took ashes to the train station. There we learned two things: First, that people are hungry for a moment of the sacred in the midst of the ordinary, and second, that doing liturgy in the street is a curiosity, photogenic, and can spread virally through a community that wasn't looking for the church in the middle of their commute.

Three moments stick with me from that first Ash Wednesday at the train station: a pair of commuters hanging over the station rail, above where we were, taking photos on their phones and marveling out loud at what seemed extraordinary—the church coming out on the sidewalk in the cold; a man who went home and brought his infant granddaughter back to one of our lay volunteers because he just wanted her to be prayed for; a young man who told us that it was his second day sober and who wasn't sure what came next—but he and we recognized the deep connection of the symbol of repentance, and the Ash Wednesday prayer that God make new hearts within us, to where he was, that particular raw morning.

Two other Episcopal churches in the Chicago area independently offered something similar at commuter train stations that year; we discovered one another through news coverage, and after sharing stories of how well received the ashes were, we decided to share it with others in the Diocese of Chicago. The following year, the Diocese of Chicago offered coordinated Ashes to Go around the city and suburbs of Chicago, and from there, the movement grew, first nationally, and then internationally, as congregations who wanted to offer ministry in the community picked up resources from Ashestogo.org, the website I launched to share resources, and from other groups that had been doing Ash Wednesday outreach for many years.

Most of the people who received ashes from us the first year were folks who were very familiar with the tradition of Ash Wednesday in the church and were delighted to find such a convenient way to engage with a symbol of faith. They wanted to receive ashes, or wear ashes through their day, but couldn't get to a service at their own church, given their work schedule. Many folks gave us very odd looks or were clearly worried that we meant to preach at them. Lots of people ignored us. Over several more years of offering Ashes to Go, more and more people received ashes, talked to us a bit more, and began to find us a normal part of their commute. That made us safer to talk to for people who didn't already know what the vestments and ashes represented, and over a few years, a number of people unfamiliar with the tradition of Ash Wednesday learned a bit about it from us—to find a public expression of faith, or an opportunity to pray for repentance and renewal, appealing. People began to say, "I'm so glad you're here!"

I've heard stories from friends offering Ashes to Go and had a number of encounters myself in which a window for profound prayer is opened. I've prayed with people on their way to surgery, struggling with broken relationships, grieving a loss that doesn't fit easy categories or struggling with a decision—people who don't have ready access to a church congregation and pastor. There are lots of reasons for that: some people just don't make a personal connection with a church they regularly attend; others have been actively injured by the church; some have drifted away out of boredom, or because the church doesn't practice what it preaches in ways important to this individual. Others have almost never been in a church.

In that way, Ashes to Go is similar to many other types of pastoral presence—an open table at a coffee shop, a prayer board on the sidewalk, a booth at a local Pride festival or farmers' market. The church coming out from behind our walls to meet people where they are—in daily business or in the concerns and celebrations that don't start in church—really makes a difference in access to the resources of prayer, community, and faith.

In my case, experiencing a positive response to Ashes to Go led me to offer the local vet a service to support people grieving a pet, which eventually grew into an ecumenical annual memorial and pet blessing. There, too, the church came out of our own "territory," metaphorically and physically, and met people in one of the places we often connect with love, and the spiritual power of life and death but don't always know how to connect with our faith. The church is, very definitely, not God, but by going into places where the church doesn't usually show up, people may experience an unexpected encounter with the church as God showing up for them in ordinary and unexpected places, places where we may need that sense of God's presence much more than we need it in the church building.

I think one of the reasons Ashes to Go is popular is because it's something that's easy to take outside the church. Ashes are a very portable symbol, and they are embedded in a ritual that will do much of the work for us. We don't need to invent an activity to take to the community, nor do we have to craft a liturgy from scratch for a "secular" need. The tools are all right there for the church that desires to offer something to the community. And the symbol and ritual allow people who encounter Ashes to Go to access sacred presence and meaning without having to start with conversation and explanations when those feel awkward.

Plus, it's photogenic and arouses curiosity, which allows people who don't directly engage to experience something of the church showing up in the world; people may connect with the experience without ever receiving ashes or share the encounter with folks who aren't physically there.

I think there's another particularly special thing about Ashes to Go, in taking what might seem to be the least marketable part of our tradition out to "the streets." Every February or March, I stand in some public place and essentially remind people we're going to die. And we "lament our sins and acknowledge our wretchedness" in prayer—in a public place, where we're usually responsible for demonstrating our worthiness and competence or at least keeping up the appearance that we're not broken. I'm sure that makes some people uncomfortable, even as they are glad to receive the ashes and wear them because they are steeped in years of tradition and faith. But I've come to suspect that we increasingly need these opportunities to acknowledge failure, brokenness, incompetence in the face of trouble too big for us, or trouble of our own making. We need to acknowledge our wretchedness—our unhappy inability to save ourselves—so that we can hang onto our sanity in a world that tends to insist we should be saving ourselves, in spite of systemic challenges none of us can solve alone. It's a relief, in a relentlessly success-oriented world, to acknowledge we're broken, and mortal—and then we get to open ourselves to grace. Praying about that in public, with a hundred and more people in a few hours every year, has fundamentally changed my own habits of acknowledging brokenness in my daily life and faith, and increased my own sense of my and our dependence on God as a gift, not a failure.

I also love that Ashes to Go helps enable people to be witnesses of faith as they go on through their daily rounds. For folks who want to wear their faith on their faces on this special day when tradition encourages that, ashes to go can make that witness accessible to people whose schedule or whose relationship with the institution of the church would otherwise prevent them.

Sacred Ground curriculum: Learn more at episcopalchurch.org/sacred-ground/

Supplemental Reading

Being Christian: Baptism, Bible, Eucharist, Prayer by Rowan Williams (Eerdmans, 2014)

Being Disciples: Essentials of the Christian Life by Rowan Williams (Eerdmans, 2016)

The Bible Tells Me So: Uses and Abuses of Holy Scripture by Jim Hill (Anchor, 1995)

Canoeing the Mountain: Christian Leadership in Uncharted Territory by Tod Bolsinger (IVP Books, 2015)

The Church Cracked Open: Disruption, Decline, and New Hope for Beloved Community by Stephanie Spellers (Church Publishing, 2021)

From Values to Action: The Four Principles of Values-Based Leadership by Harry M. Kraemer Jr. (Jossey-Bass, 2011)

The Heart of a Leader: Saint Paul as Mentor, Model, and Encourager by Edward S. Little (Forward Movement, 2020)

Life Together: The Classic Exploration of Christian in Community by Dietrich Bonhoeffer (HarperOne, 1978)

Jesus and the Disinherited by Howard Thurman (Beacon Press, Reprint edition, 1996)

Jesus Was An Episcopalian (And You Can Be One Too!): A Newcomer's Guide to the Episcopal Church by Chris Yaw (LeaderResources, 2008)

People of the Way: Renewing Episcopal Identity by Dwight Zscheile (Morehouse Publishing, 2012)

Radical Welcome: Embracing God, the Other, and the Spirit of Transformation by Stephanie Spellers, (Church Publishing, 2006)

Rise: Bold Strategies to Transform Your Church by Callie Parkinson (NavPress, 2015).

The Sabbath by Abraham Joshua Heschel (Farrar Straus Giroux; Illustrated edition, 2005)

Shaped by the Bible by William Willimon (Abingdon Press, Underlining edition, 1991)

Tempered Resilience: How Leaders Are Formed in the Crucible of Change by Tod Bolsinger (IVP Books, 2020)

The Way of Love: A Practical Guide to Following Jesus by Scott Gunn (Forward Movement, 2020)

Acknowledgments

This book is offered in thanksgiving for generous donors who made the work of RenewalWorks possible. You know who you are.

About the Author

Jay Sidebotham has served as a priest in the Episcopal Church for more than 30 years, blessed to have served congregations in Rhode Island, New York City, Washington, D.C, suburban Chicago, and several communities in North Carolina. He has also enjoyed creating artwork, including cartoons, reflecting life in the Episcopal Church. (The church provides so much material!) The illustrations represent continuity with the work he did prior to ordination, first working in  an animation studio that produced *Schoolhouse Rock* cartoons, and then as an art director in several advertising agencies. Some say he is still in advertising.

About Forward Movement

Forward Movement inspires disciples and empowers evangelists. While we produce great resources like this book, Forward Movement is not a publishing company. We are a discipleship ministry. We live out this ministry through creating and publishing books, daily reflections, studies for small groups, and online resources. People around the world read daily devotions through *Forward Day by Day*, which is also available in Spanish (*Adelante Dia a Dia*) and Braille, online, as a podcast, and as an app for smartphones.

We actively seek partners across the church and look for ways to provide resources that inspire and challenge. A ministry of the Episcopal Church since 1935, Forward Movement is a nonprofit organization funded by sales of resources and gifts from generous donors.

To learn more about Forward Movement and our work, visit us at ForwardMovement.org or VenAdelante.org. We are delighted to be doing this work and invite your prayers and support.